"Instead of running away (have you roaring like a lion ᴀᴛ ᴛʜᴇ ᴍᴏꜱᴛ ꜱɪɢʜ ᴏꜰ ꜰᴇᴀʀ — ᴀɴᴅ ᴛʜᴇɴ the devil will be running in fear!"

Sid Roth, host, *It's Supernatural!*

"*Slaying the Giant of Fear* is a battle cry for the Body of Christ! Giants will be slain, mountains will be moved and breakthrough will come to the readers of this powerful book! It is time to be empowered by the authority you have been given through Jesus. Your strategy to overcome is here!"

Sula Skiles, pastor, author and sex trafficking abolitionist, www.sulaskiles.com

"I believe this book! I believe that it is possible to slay the giant of fear! In your hands, you hold a masterfully crafted plan of action on how to do it. I especially love that at the end of each chapter, Krissy Nelson gives us a declaration to help us seal the revelation that we have received. If you rise up to the challenge and walk through the steps that she has laid out for you, I believe the results will exceed your expectations! Get ready to release your roar of breakthrough as you read this awesome book!"

Joshua Mills, bestselling author of *Moving in Glory Realms* and *Seeing Angels*, www.joshuamills.com

"Fear can be a bully even with the strongest woman. *Slaying the Giant of Fear* leads us from our own strength to step into faith that calms and conquers that bully."

Suzanne Eller, bestselling author and co-host of *More Than Small Talk* podcast

"Do you struggle with fear? We all have at some point in our lives! *Slaying the Giant of Fear* will help you victoriously overcome fear and gain momentum again. God has destined you to live a life of radical faith that is free from being crippled by fear. It is time!"

Ana Werner, founder, Ana Werner Ministries, www.anawerner.org

"Let's face it—we all have fears. Some are real and some are imagined. Some can cause us to hesitate, while others may literally paralyze us or even control our lives. Krissy has beautifully shared with us how to identify and deal with the fears that hold us back. It is not about avoiding fear but pressing through, facing it and overcoming it. She teaches us that *we* can choose not to allow fear to intimidate, consume or direct our steps. God controls the outcome of our lives, not our circumstances! I highly recommend this excellent book *Slaying the Giant of Fear*."

Pastor Mave Moyer, co-founder, Eagle Worldwide Ministries

"Wow! What a wonderfully written book! *Slaying the Giant of Fear* is full of insights that will empower you to remove the giants that intimidate you. Crafted to create a God-confidence in your life, this book will deliver! Read it from cover to cover and hear the heart of a woman who has overcome fear."

Brian Simmons, The Passion Translation Project

"Krissy Nelson's book *Slaying the Giant of Fear* is a gift from the heart of God for this new era. It is a sword of revelation given from the Lord to see His people rise up to a place of deep adoration for their God, standing boldly knowing who is with them, who goes before them, who lives in them and whose they are. This book will not only change your life, it will activate you into a new level of bold faith and no toleration for fear. It carries an impartation for deliverance from the stronghold of fear and will plunge you into the depths of His love and ignite within you His spirit of adventure with Jesus, taking you into new lands that are part of your destiny. I not only highly recommend this book to you but also my dear friend Krissy Nelson, who is not only so special to me but also a friend of God."

Lana Vawser, author, speaker and prophetic voice, Lana Vawser Ministries, www.lanavawser.com

"My friend Krissy Nelson has done it again! With the courage of vulnerability and her finely tuned ear to the voice of the

Holy Spirit, she guides you step-by-step from anxiety to peace, insecurity to confidence, timidity to bravery. This is your must-have manual for breakthrough!"

"In this strategic guidebook, Krissy Nelson equips you to walk in your identity and destiny like David did: trained for battle, courageous and full of faith. Krissy overcame fear to be a voice. There are God promises for your life, too. The world needs you, Beloved—it is time to shine!"

"As I write this endorsement, the nations are reeling in the throes of a global pandemic. The look in people's eyes behind their protective face masks is absolutely heartbreaking. They are afraid like they've never been afraid before. Much like Krissy details in her book *Slaying the Giant of Fear*, you won't escape great opportunities to be afraid. It is what you do with the fear that counts. Krissy's book is an absolutely victorious read. Read it and slay the giant of fear in your life for good."

"I believe fear is one of the greatest spirits attacking the Body of Christ today. When you read this book, I really believe revelation will come upon you and the lies and torment of fear will be broken off you. Krissy, thank you for boldly addressing a subject that few people have really broken free from. This book will be a light for many generations to follow!"

SLAYING the
GIANT
of FEAR

SLAYING the
GIANT
of FEAR

AND RELEASING THE ROAR
OF BREAKTHROUGH

KRISSY NELSON

Chosen

a division of Baker Publishing Group
Minneapolis, Minnesota

© 2020 by Krissy Nelson

Published by Chosen Books
11400 Hampshire Avenue South
Bloomington, Minnesota 55438
www.chosenbooks.com

Chosen Books is a division of
Baker Publishing Group, Grand Rapids, Michigan

Printed in the United States of America

Library of Congress Cataloging-in-Publication Data
Names: Nelson, Krissy, author.
Title: Slaying the giant of fear: and releasing the roar of breakthrough / Krissy Nelson.
Description: Bloomington, Minnesota: Bethany House Publishers, 2020.
Identifiers: LCCN 2020011356 | ISBN 9780800799663 (trade paperback) | ISBN 9781493424856 (ebook)
Subjects: LCSH: Fear—Religious aspects—Christianity.
Classification: LCC BV4908.5 .N448 2020 | DDC 248.8/6—dc23
LC record available at https://lccn.loc.gov/2020011356

In some cases, the names of individuals and identifying details have been changed to protect privacy.

20 21 22 23 24 25 26   7 6 5 4 3 2 1

To my children:

my daughter, Jenessa, and my son, Justice

Never forget how much Jesus loves you
and the giant of fear fears you.
Roar your roar of breakthrough
and take the land God has given you.
You are champions in Christ.

Contents

Foreword

Krissy Nelson is a wife and mother as well as innovative mover and shaker. She is paving the way for a new generation to break out of a structure of fear into freedom and fulfillment. I have loved the times of connecting with Krissy and her family. I call them real people. I love her passion for God and the intensity of her God-given purpose and mandate. She is willing to step out of the box called "ordinary."

Reading her book jumpstarted me on a reminiscing trip over past experiences I have had with fear. Her experiences also reminded me of others who have shared their journey of overcoming fear. Then there was that book I wrote, *Taking On Goliath*, about giants in our lives. Memories rushed into my mind as I reviewed her book.

Fear is one of the main forces—if not the main force—that creates seemingly impossible barriers to our fulfilling God's plan for our lives. Fear attempts to stop specific assignments He has given us and steps of obedience we need to take that seem beyond the ordinary.

This is not new. The Israelites faced inordinate fear when God invited them to go into Canaan and possess it, bit by bit, for themselves. Nearly all the original children of Israel were disqualified from entering the Promised Land because, in the war between fear and faith, they gave themselves over to fear. I believe this is the exact issue we are facing today as God has given us the opportunity to turn nations around and to transform our own lives and the lives of those we influence.

When I had just completed graduate school, the university invited me, because of my academic record, to join the staff as a professor. My very first assignment was to teach Ph.D.s who would be flying in from all over the United States to attend a four-week seminar in my area of expertise. But I was wet behind the ears, a total newbie. What did I have to give them? I was terrified!

The night before my first lecture, I was panic-stricken. I could not sleep. My stomach was rolling and making strange sounds. My skin crawled. Everything in my body seemed to shout *terror!* Finally I turned on the light and began to read desperately through the Psalms, starting with the very first one. I must have read halfway through the book screaming silently, *God, please help me!* Finally I came to a verse that broke the tyranny of my panic. Fear changed to faith. Releasing a humongous sigh of relief, I turned off the light and went to sleep. The next day I taught those educated professors with confidence. I went beyond my fear into faith, beyond my ability into God's supernatural ability. I decimated a Goliath.

We are in a "go-beyond" time. God is challenging us today to go beyond our comfort zones, abilities and previous achievements to do things that directly challenge our fears. He is inviting us to partner with Him to discover fresh and deeper faith—not just our own faith, but to move out of fear to access His faith. If we are true New Testament believers, then we must become a supernatural people who do the impossible, a people who go beyond.

Krissy Nelson not only addresses fear but provides excellent examples of what fear looks like, how it talks to us and what its goal is. It is a Goliath that wants to paralyze us in a frozen place. Furthermore she challenges us to "go beyond" and replace fear with faith. And she lays out a biblical strategy on how to do this.

We have entered an era that is not easy. The days ahead will be filled with opportunities for us to freeze in terror. But if we overcome, we must replace those "now" fears by moving into audacious faith—faith that rises up to navigate impossible times and tasks.

Barbara J. Yoder, lead apostle and founding pastor,
Shekinah Regional Apostolic Center,
Ann Arbor, Michigan

Introduction

Not long ago I found myself on the cusp of significant breakthrough in my life. For the first time, I felt ready to step fully into the destiny I knew God had planned for me. I could see it, see Him, beckoning to me to walk forward and claim the promised land He had been preparing for me for so long. Yet at the same time I was paralyzed with fear. Instead of admitting my fear of the future to the Lord, I clammed up in an attempt to remain strong and courageous. I had succumbed to the wrong assumption that being afraid was a sign of weakness and doubt, so confessing I was scared—me, an author, television host and ministry leader—felt like exposing myself as a fraud. I told myself I should be immune to fear, that if my faith were strong enough, I would not be dealing with these feelings, right? The building pressure had become nearly unbearable. I was in agony. I could feel the roar of breakthrough rising within me, but when I opened my mouth to release it, to release the pressure, all that came out was a whimper.

Can you relate to this feeling? I know you can, because I know that everyone is afraid sometimes. Everyone. You are not alone, and you are certainly not faithless or a fraud or weak because of it.

Friend, it is time to admit your own reasons right here for justifying the expectation that you should be immune to fear. It is time to be honest and real. It might seem strange now, but as you will see in this book, being transparent about your fear is the first step you will take toward your destiny. It is exactly the action that will turn your whimper into a roar that can shake the gates of hell. Trust me; I speak from experience.

Truth That Calms the Storm

Eventually the pressure behind my fear became so strong that I could no longer ignore it. I could not stuff my feelings anymore because there was simply nowhere left to hide them. In my little room, on my knees before God, I bent down in defeat.

Like Peter, I had stepped out of the boat, but when I looked behind me all I could see were the impossible waters I had crossed over thus far. I wondered, how could I continue to follow Jesus atop the water? How could I maintain a lifestyle of radical faith in order to walk forward further and further from the boat, no land in sight, when I was frozen in terror? I could barely hear Jesus's voice saying, "Come," over the sound of the storm. My weakness as a human being was painfully obvious next to Him. I knew that I faced a new choice: Continue forward in faith, or surrender to the fear of the unknown.

I could almost feel the wind blowing all around me. In my mind's eye I began to look down at the surface of the water. Every limitation I had, every struggle and every doubt rose like a giant wave trying to take me down. The storm carried a voice shouting at me to quit right then and there. It said, "You're not good enough. You can't do this. You didn't get here on your own. You should quit now."

Yes, the enemy seized the opportunity to dictate the narrative of my life. His voice thundered around me, even speaking into the steps I had already taken with the Lord and attempting to pervert where God had taken me: out into the deep of the impossible realm of His Kingdom. He twisted the truth with his accusations and lies, reminding me I never could have gotten where I was on my own. And he was right about that; God had gotten me where I was.

Fear began to come over me. I wanted to turn around and run back toward the boat. I wanted to throw in the towel. What God had put before me was too big. It was way bigger than I could have imagined, and I was painfully aware that I could not do it. No way. No how.

That was when the lightbulb of truth came on. Suddenly the waves stopped and the wind was silenced as truth came crashing in. It was so obvious that I wondered why I had not been clinging to this truth all along: Whatever God calls you to do for Him will always be bigger than you. It will always seem impossible. It will always feel as though you are stepping farther and farther into the deep without a map and only Jesus as your guide. He will go before you and hold your hand, all at the same time. Jesus will lock eyes with you, speaking truth and encouragement. *Fear not*, He will tell you. *You can do this. I am with you. Nothing is impossible with God.*

Finally I could hear His voice over the sound of the wind and the crashing water. I suddenly got it. I understood the supernatural reality of this life of faith we are called to walk as disciples of Christ Jesus, our Lord. I began to accept the new normal of life outside the boat with Jesus—never dull, never predictable and always an adventure of faith.

From the depths of my soul I pressed past the lies of the enemy and cried to the Father, admitting my fear. "God, I'm scared." As these words left my lips, a roar swelled from the inside of me. Now my heavenly Father was dictating the narrative of my life all over again, and not the giant of fear. Once again I allowed my admission of fear to exit my soul, this time as a shout of hope that something would be different. "I'm scared, Abba!"

I felt a weight lift from my shoulders. The cry of truth thundering from the depths of my soul was a roar of break-through in my life. Just as a lion paralyzes its prey with the sound of its roar, fear was paralyzed by the sound bellowing out of me, and the giant fell silent on the sidelines.

In the silence, the Father spoke. His words were simple, pure and piercing. He said, "Krissy, I never leave My sheep without a Shepherd."

You see, no matter the call, Jesus is with you. He is your great Shepherd. The Bible says, "I will never leave you or forsake you" (Hebrews 13:5). Jesus paid it all so that you could live your days on this earth filled with His presence and power to do the impossible.

You Can Be Fearless

We all experience fear at some point for different reasons. And guess what. That is okay. The goal is not avoiding fear.

The goal is pressing forward despite fear. It is us focusing more on Jesus than on the giant of fear. The truth is, in our humanity, we all have weakness and limitations. But instead of us coming into agreement with the giant of fear and saying, "Yeah, I'm weak. I should just go back to the boat until I'm stronger," we can remind ourselves we are filled with the same Spirit that raised Christ from the dead (Romans 8:11). We can proclaim, as Paul did, "I will boast in my weakness, because it is in my weakness that His power is made perfect" (2 Corinthians 11:30; 12:9). This is such good news, my friend. You can reframe your weaknesses and limitations so they are not areas where you feel ashamed but instead guideposts of just how much you need Jesus every single day.

What a gift that is, recognizing our dependency on Christ. "'For it is not by power nor might, but by My Spirit,' says the Lord," according to the Scriptures (Zechariah 4:6). We all need Jesus. Every single day we need Him. It is in Him we live and move and have our being. It is in Him we are strong. He is our good Shepherd, leading us through our life and rescuing us from the mouth of the bear and the paw of the lion. Just as a human shepherd rescues his sheep, so Jesus rescues us from the teeth of the enemy's lies and accusations.

Allow Him to rescue you right now. And let out a shout! "Jesus, I need you!" Give it a try right now, will you? Let out a roar from within and declare, "Thank You, Jesus, that I am weak! Thank You for this ever-present reminder that it is Your strength I need more of and not my own!"

We must realize that since we are God's sheep, He will never leave us without a Shepherd. Because He is watching over you, you can be bold and courageous. You can be fearless. You do not have to wait for someone else to prepare the way. Jesus already prepared the way. He *is* the way! And His Spirit will lead you, like the Shepherd that He is, right across the victory line where the giant of fear tried to defeat you.

Ready to Roar

As God began to reveal to me the weapons I would need in order to take down the giant of fear, I began to see David and Goliath's face-off in a new light and understand the supernatural pearls of truth God embedded within this story. Given what God revealed to me about the significance of His role as our good Shepherd, it should come as no surprise that the Lord would use a human shepherd to teach us an important lesson about His own Shepherd's heart for us and how to rely on Him to defeat the giant of fear forever.

In this book, I will teach you exactly what God taught me, and continues to teach me, through David's story. We will step together up to the battle line alongside David to learn what it was that made him victorious. We will see why David did not fear men, not even a giant, and we will learn how to ignore the voice of the enemy, as he did.

We will also look at the weapons David used to defeat the giant of fear before he ever faced off with Goliath. God has given us the same weapons—obedience, faithfulness and stewardship—and you will be encouraged to know you already have them in your arsenal. You just have to learn how to use them to slay the giant of fear.

As you come into agreement with all the Lord has for you, you will take your stand in opposition to fear. The giant's voice will have less say in your life as the voice of God grows louder and more profound. By the end, you will find yourself roaring your roar of breakthrough, paralyzing the giant of fear as he bows to the name of Jesus, while you run victoriously across the battle line and into the destiny God has planned for you. It may seem hard to believe now, but your freedom from fear is coming.

My friend, I know firsthand how debilitating fear can be. But there is hope. Right now the deep in me is calling out to the deep in you. As we travel together through this book, you will begin to identify and sharpen the weapons given to you by God Almighty. You will learn about God's plan for your life, a plan that includes freedom from the grip of fear, and how to cut off the head of the giant of fear, just as David did. Most importantly, you will come to know you have been lovingly equipped for every battle you will ever face by a God who has already assured you the victory. You do not have to fight and strive anymore, only to find yourself bruised and battered but no closer to the promised land. All you have to do is take the first step and let God unfold the rest.

Are you ready? Let's get started.

PART 1

THE GIANT
EXPOSED

1

The Problem

Then the Philistine said, "This day I defy the armies of Israel! Give me a man and let us fight each other." On hearing the Philistine's words, Saul and all the Israelites were dismayed and terrified.

1 Samuel 17:10–11

One giant stood at the battle line calling out to the army of the Lord and causing them to run away in terror. "Why do you come out and line up for battle? Am I not a Philistine, and are you not the servants of Saul?" (1 Samuel 17:8). His taunts echoed across the valley floor, striking fear in the hearts of an entire army and their king.

Can you imagine? You are all geared up for battle. You are surrounded by an army of soldiers ready to fight, but out of nowhere a terrifying adversary walks right out of your worst nightmare and into the landscape before you. Fear begins to swell up from deep within. And then he speaks. A sound like a roar is released from this giant's mouth as he declares your doomed fate. His words crush your destiny and challenge everything you believe in, even your trust in God.

His bold, booming threats fill your heart with panic. You look to your right and to your left to find your fellow army mates with that same pale look of terror on their faces. Then all at once the whole company of soldiers turns and runs the other direction from the foe. You follow.

For forty days this giant Goliath stood at the battle line taunting the Israelites to find even one brave man willing to rise up and fight. Morning and night, he came out shouting the same intimidating challenge: "This day I defy the armies of Israel! Give me a man and let us fight each other" (1 Samuel 17:10).

Not one could be found who would fight this giant, not even King Saul, who, the Bible says, had no equal and was a head taller than any of the others (1 Samuel 9:2). Even with his physical stature, fear consumed the king, and Saul ran away in fear right alongside his army. Each morning they gathered at the battle line, the giant on one side, King Saul and the army on the other. And each time the Bible says every one of God's people ran away "dismayed and terrified" (1 Samuel 17:11).

This is what fear does. Fear challenges our faith. It strikes panic in our heart until we can barely move, except to flee from the battle line and away from our destiny. But fear need not rule your life anymore.

Your Response to Fear

The story of David and Goliath is filled with wisdom to help us walk in victory over fear. For one, it helps us clarify our response to fear and develop new patterns of behavior.

Have you ever wondered why fear so often causes us to question our very identity, as well as the identity of the One who fights our battles? Deuteronomy 3:22 (ESV) says, "You shall not fear them, for it is the LORD your God who fights for you," yet we still fear. We still struggle to trust that the Lord is going to battle on our behalf. Like the Israelites, we crumble under the weight of dismay.

The Hebrew word for "dismay," *chathath*,* speaks to a shattering that occurs. In that brokenness, courage and resolution are lost, seemingly forever. Before the giant Goliath, an army who by nature should have been full of courage—they were numerous, they were trained, they had a leader and, most importantly, they were God's army—came apart. Such intense feelings for an army of men. How could this be? How could one giant cause an entire army to retreat in fear like this, to back down from their God-given mandate to take the land?

Shattered from Within

The reality is, fear is relentless. Even with just a few little words the enemy can amplify the sound of fear in our hearts, causing us to retreat in panic. Then the spirit of fear calls out to us from within, as Goliath called out to the army: "This day I defy you. Give me one man or woman who will dare fight me." We can count on fear to shout menacingly at us from the battle line of our life at four times our size and adorned in seemingly impenetrable armor. We can count on our flesh to run and hide. It will do it every time.

*Biblehub.com, s.v. "*chathath*."

29

In the story of David and Goliath, the Israelite army is a symbol of the flesh, and David is a symbol of the spirit. What is the difference between flesh and spirit? That answer could fill the pages of another book, but to put it simply: Our spirit is that place within us that responds to God's Spirit. It bears witness to the truth and to what is right. Our flesh is our carnal nature. It will often lead us into sin, doubt, fear and more. When faith is challenged, the flesh responds automatically with fear. Through preparation and prayer, however, we can learn to use fear as a trigger to tell our spirit to rise up and fight through the power of God's Spirit at work within us, as He was with David.

That is what you are doing with this book. Together we will practice identifying the giant of fear and then overriding your flesh's response to it so that your spirit can take over. Romans 8:5 (ESV) tells us, "For those who live according to the flesh set their minds on the things of the flesh, but those who live according to the Spirit set their minds on the things of the Spirit." You will practice positioning yourself so you can take a stance like David, one that can see fear for what it is: a defiant giant that dares defy the powerful armies of the living God. We will also practice wielding the three most powerful supernatural weapons God has given us in our fight against fear: obedience, faithfulness and stewardship.

David embodied the truth that God does not give us "a spirit of fear, but of power and of love and of a sound mind" (2 Timothy 1:7 NKJV). By the end of this book, you will do the same so that you can approach the battle line with the proper perspective, positioning and supernatural weapons to slay the giant once and for all!

David: A Symbol of the Spirit

David is known as a man after God's heart (1 Samuel 13:14). When we encounter his story in the Scriptures, David is a shepherd boy serving his family, working in the fields, and the youngest of eight sons. While he was not the oldest among his brothers, he was given the mantle of firstborn by God Himself (see Psalm 89:27).

David was such a faithful shepherd that when he went to serve his brothers at the battlefield, he left his sheep with another shepherd so they would not be unattended (1 Samuel 17:20). Can't you just see the heart of God even in this simple act of David caring for his sheep? He would never leave them alone. Even David's sheep did not need to be afraid, for there was always a good shepherd nearby caring for them and looking after them.

While David had never experienced battle, as a shepherd guarding sheep he was familiar with danger. God had saved him from the paw of the lion and the paw of the bear, and he knew God as his protector. This powerful, trusting relationship with God was the foundation for his encounter with Goliath.

David entered the battlefield bearing food he brought for his brothers. Standing among the army, he overheard the taunts of the Philistine warrior giant, and instead of retreating in fear like the rest of them, David was appalled at his mockery. He looked to the soldiers standing near him and asked, "What will be done for the man who kills this Philistine and removes this disgrace from Israel? Who is this uncircumcised Philistine that should defy the armies of the living God?" (verse 26).

This young man who had no experience on the field of battle could have been terrified by the sight of Goliath, as

31

was the entire army of Israel, but David knew who would fight the battle through him. He walked in fellowship with the Lord and knew intimately the protection of Jehovah-Nissi—God my Banner—who had delivered him from the paw of the bear and the lion while he was guarding the sheep (verse 37). He knew he had no reason to fear this taunting giant directly mocking the armies of the living God because the Lord would fight for him.

For forty days Goliath had been spewing out carnal threats, tearing away at the army's confidence in God. Remember how immediately Goliath identified them as the "servants of Saul" in 1 Samuel 17:8? They were really the army of the living God, not just the army of any human king. By redirecting the soldiers' faith in God to faith in their human king, Goliath managed to splinter and then shatter the army's confidence. Fear had tightened its noose.

But David could not be swayed. Victory over this giant was not a question for David. Because of his relationship with God, he was not thrown off by the giant's lies and distortions of truth. He knew to whom he belonged, and he knew his foe was in direct violation and defiance of almighty God. He was led by the Spirit of God and not by his flesh, so he operated with a deep, inward assurance. The sounds of fear were not amplified within him, only the deep, inward confidence in the Lord almighty. Therefore, running away in fear was not an option, and he was baffled at the sight of this army who had great fear.

You, too, can have this kind of assurance. When the giant of fear stands at the battle line of victory in your life, be assured God will fight for you. He activates supernatural weapons you may not even realize you have. They may seem dull now, but they will become progressively sharper through your daily walk with the Lord. Through the fire and through the rain, as you depend on God, He will ease your pain. He will fight for you. He will win every war. He will hold you by the hand and remind you who you are and whose you are. Eventually, when you stand before a fearsome adversary, you will not wither and run in fear. Instead, you will charge boldly into battle like David, knowing the war has already been fought and won for you by your Father in heaven, through Jesus' victory on the cross.

A New Mom Battles Fear

I will never forget the night fear woke me up. Gasping for breath, I shot straight up in my bed. The clock read 2:00 a.m. I looked down at my newborn baby fast asleep in her bassinet on my left. To my right was my husband, who was also fast asleep. A sense of relief came over me as I saw my loud gasp for air had not awakened either of them.

There in the dark I began to think about the days that were fast approaching. I was only three weeks postpartum and facing my dreaded return to work. Gazing down at my new baby, I wondered how other working moms did it. This was all new to me, and the thought of leaving my newborn with strangers terrified me.

I had never known fear like that before. On one hand, returning to work seemed so simple, but on the other hand, I was overwhelmed by the unknown. The internal tension I was experiencing was so intense. A once career-minded, ladder-climbing young woman, now I was transformed by this little life lying peacefully next to me. Instead of planning ways to advance my career, I found myself wondering, *What am I doing with my life?*

That night, tears began to fall from my eyes, and a silent cry came from deep within. I began to tremble, as I was trying so hard not to let my cries be heard. The more I wept, the more I began to wonder if I could ever go back. I was terrified at leaving my baby girl, frightened that I no longer wanted the things in my career I had worked so hard to build, and overwhelmed at the thought of all the people who were relying on me to return to work as the same person I had left just a few weeks prior.

I had my dream job to look forward to, yet here I was trembling in fear at the thought of going back. I had just helped a good friend of mine realize her ambition of owning her own women's health club. She had put everything on the line to pursue her dream and trusted me to be her operations manager. She was depending on me to help her run with it all.

I was very driven in those days. I remember being in labor standing over my hospital bed with my laptop, notebook and cell phone all sprawled out before me on the bed. It was the wee hours of the morning, and between contractions I was frantically sending out final e-mails to candidates I had interviewed in the days prior, letting them know they did or did not get the job. I needed to tie up these loose ends so they could begin their training and I could go on and have a baby.

My daughter was born on February 21, and the luxurious new women's health club we worked tirelessly to build was scheduled to open just a few weeks later. Prior to having a baby I could not fathom how or why moms needed more than a couple weeks off work after baby, and boy, was I in for a surprise!

In the dark, my daughter at my side, I sat thinking about everyone who was counting on me to be on top of my game in just about a week. In my mind's eye I saw the faces of all the people who would look to me for leadership. I imagined the phone calls coming in day and night with questions, and the glitches that would no doubt occur with all the new equipment, security system, computer software, etc. The weight of all of this was overwhelming. And I broke.

You want to know what my greatest fear was? Even though I loved my work, I suddenly no longer wanted any of it. That thought alone terrified me. Instead of excitement at the thought of getting back in the swing of things, I felt trapped by my job, when all I really wanted to do was be at home raising my daughter. To make matters worse, some of my own dreams were beginning to surface again, dreams I would never have time to pursue if I was raising my daughter and working full-time.

On top of those fears, I worried about letting people down, especially my friend and boss. She was relying on me to return as the same person who had left before having my baby, and there I sat in the dark of my room wondering who that person even was anymore.

At that point I could no longer contain the sound of my sobs. My husband shot straight up and immediately wrapped his arm around me. At first he struggled to form words but finally put together the obvious question: "What happened? Is everyone okay?"

Weeping and nodding my head that yes, everyone was all right, I managed to form a short sentence. "I don't want to go back to work," I told him. I was finally willing to admit it. My words trailed off as if there was so much more to say but no energy left to say it. Deep, guttural cries from within began bellowing out of me.

I was no longer the person I had grown to know. In a lot of ways that was a good thing. I was going to be better for it, certainly, because I had grown quite selfish. But at the same time I was terrified of who I was becoming. The new me had totally different dreams and plans from what I had known and wanted before. In a matter of moments I had gone from loving my dream job to feeling as if I was a slave to money and other people's expectations, and that appeared to be my new normal. I felt stuck, like I had no options. It only got worse as time went on.

When I returned to work there were many days I would sneak to the back of the building in the alleyway and just cry. I did not want to be there. My efforts not to disappoint anyone seemed fractured, and I was certain I was letting everyone down. I was not able to be the mom I wanted to be, home nurturing my brand-new baby, and I was not able to be the coworker or leader I wanted to be because I was so distracted by my emotions and the deep changes that had occurred within me. I was juggling disappointment on all fronts, including with myself for not being able to juggle both career and family at the same time. I knew I needed to pull the trigger on the decision that seemed so obvious: to lay down my career.

Finally, after about six months, I was able to choose family and walk away from the career I once loved. While I still continued to work, I was able to find a nine-to-five job that let me leave the office and be all-in with my family when I was home. I realized I was not stuck and did not need to live under the fear of other people's expectations anymore, even if it meant doing the unpopular thing. I was not going to live in fear any longer—not fear of failure, fear of rejection, fear of not having enough, none of it. God was calling me home. He had course-corrected my life, and I was going to go after Him.

This was the beginning of my journey in identifying, battling and defeating fear. There was so much I did not know and so much I could have done differently. Looking back, I wish I knew then what I know now. But deciding to fight fear—even if I did not yet know how—was a pivotal moment in my life. It is what brought me here, and it helped shape what I will share in this book in the hope that you will not make the same mistakes I did.

Where are you in your journey with fear, my friend? Whether your toes are on the battle line for the first time, or you have run away and returned over and over again, you need to know there is freedom and victory over fear. So take a deep breath of relief. There is hope on the horizon, because God does not send us out without equipping us first. You do not have to be afraid anymore. The supernatural weapons you will be able to use to defeat fear are in your hands and heart right now as you read. You will soon learn how they work in tandem together to give you long-term victory over the Goliath in front of you.

DECLARE IT

Father, thank You for giving me everything I need to defeat the power of fear in my life. I am ready. I am a champion in Christ!

2

When Fear Gets
the Upper Hand

Be alert and of sober mind. Your enemy the devil
prowls around like a roaring lion looking for
someone to devour.

1 Peter 5:8

It was the middle of my seventh-grade year, and I had just
switched from the public school I grew up attending to
a new private school. In reality it was not that far away,
but it felt like I had been shipped off to another continent.
I knew no one, and I was certain I would never convince
anyone to talk to me, much less be my friend.

As I walked down the hallway on my first day at my new
middle school, taunting thoughts crashed in my head. *See,
nobody likes you. You don't fit in. You're all alone.* It was
unbearable.

I have yet to meet someone who says they enjoyed their middle school years. It is a highly sensitive and impressionable season in our human development anyway. Then add in the need to make new friends and the fact that by that time in my life I was already deeply insecure and full of fear, and I was in agony.

I struggled to fit in almost instantly. My fears and insecurities only intensified as I fought to feel accepted. I remember one boy asking me why I was not as pretty as one of the girls I hung out with a lot, as if I had any control over that. Before long I was convinced I was not good enough, pretty enough or even enough in general. As an only child, I just was not used to this kind of drama.

False narratives and leading questions were spiraling in my mind constantly. Fear had amplified its sound deep within my heart, and all I could hear was its roaring confirmation of my deepest insecurities playing on a constant loop. *See, nobody likes you. You don't fit in here. You are all alone.*

This is when I started running—not as a sport, mind you, but out of fear. I ran from people, schools and friends. I fled from anything and everything that scared me. By the start of eighth grade I had switched schools three times, from public school to private school, to homeschool, and back to my original public school.

I had hoped that returning to the public school I had grown up in would fix some of the social anxiety I had been experiencing. After all, I would be reuniting with kids I had grown up with. It seemed logical, at least until I walked through the front doors. I can still remember that sinking feeling of fear running up and down my veins. I had expected to experience a sense of relief, but instead the fear was instant.

I choked it down and tried my best to reconnect with my peers, but it was hard. I was genuinely excited to see some of my friends from elementary school, but it turned out that during my absence, they had become established in their core group. Try as I might, I just was not able to feel a part of it. It only confirmed my worst fears. Nobody liked me after all. I did not fit in anywhere. I really was all alone.

Instead of sticking it out and trying to make friends, I gave that school six weeks and then ran again, a fourth time, my fears chasing behind me. My dad and mom had been divorced for several years at that point, and while I was living with my mom at the time, I asked to move in with my dad so I could be zoned for a different public school district. Some of the kids from my church went there, so we hoped it would be a better fit for me. It was, at least for a few weeks.

Then it happened again. The kids scared me. Some were nice, yes, but some were mean. It did not really matter at that point what they did: the way they would look at me, talk to me, not talk to me. Like each time before, I was consumed by my insecurities and tormented by doubt. I was miserable.

Fear had gotten the upper hand yet again. It stood at the battle line of my mind shouting at me relentlessly. *I told you nobody likes you. You don't fit in anywhere. You will always be alone. You will never be accepted. You are not strong enough. You are not enough.*

I remember getting on the bus one morning and almost passing out as I scanned the faces of the kids sitting in their seats, wondering if anyone would make a place for me. The false narrative the enemy had whispered now played at full volume in my mind. I sat down quickly on the corner of a seat in the front and just prayed for the day to end.

When school let out for Christmas break I recall thinking, "I'm never going back there. Nobody likes me. I don't fit in. I don't even know who I am." To be fair, this last part was true; I had no idea who I was. I felt so alone and powerless to change my circumstances.

I can still picture the night I sat down to talk with my dad. Tears were streaming down my face as I begged, "Daddy, I don't want to go back to school. I can't." My face dropped into my hands. I did not know what was the matter with me that I could not handle school or even people. I did not understand why I felt so paralyzed by what people thought about me. Fear had gripped my little heart so tightly that it was hard to breathe.

My dad did not make me return to the school. He knew his daughter was going to be okay and that I just needed some time to get my focus off my fear and back on Jesus, so he pulled me out to homeschool me for the second time. There were some who did not understand his decision, but thankfully my dad understood that fear is fear, no matter how old you are, and took it seriously enough to give me the space to get the upper hand before it shaped my young life any further.

Not long afterward, when I was fifteen years old, I had an encounter with the Lord at a revival service in Pensacola, Florida, that interrupted fear's reign over my life, at least for a little while. The Father wrapped me in His arms and held me the entire night. He said to me, "Krissy, I've always been with you, but now I have my arms wrapped around you." All night long He spoke into my destiny, giving me revelation into His heart and nature as a good, good Father and bringing to the forefront of my mind familiar Scriptures that confirmed these truths. My Abba Father breathed on the embers of my heart, and I came alive as if for the first time! Once insecure, isolated and bound with the fear of rejection, fear of man and fear of just about everything, suddenly I knew who I was. I became bold and courageous for the Lord. That was not the end of my war with fear. Truthfully, the worst was yet to come. But that night, for the first time ever, I felt what it was like to rest in the authority of Christ. As the years went by and the battle became more intense, the comfort and revelation the Father Himself gave me that night served as a lighthouse for my soul, beckoning me to keep going and giving me hope that peace was, indeed, coming.

What Is Fear?

Fear's goal is to cripple you and keep you bound. After all, how can you be a threat to the kingdom of darkness and walk out God's plan for you when you are shackled by the limitations of your own fears? That's why fear is the devil's primary weapon in keeping us from our God-given kingdom assignments. But there is good news: God has a plan, too. His plan is to free us from fear and set us on a path of peace, love, joy and hope. That freedom begins with understanding our enemy.

My dad, Dr. James Torkildson, did not just accidentally stumble onto the solution to the crippling fear I experienced in middle school. He is a psychologist with a lifetime of experience and education on the subject of fear. This is how he describes it:

> Psychologists define *fear* as "an emotionally driven outcome that results from our brain processing danger." High levels of fear can result in extreme immobilization. It shortens

oxygen to the brain causing us to not be able to think, which creates what's called a "flight or fight" response. Fear can be highly disabling and cause one to retreat and seek isolation.

Fear can take a variety of forms, including the fear of man (i.e., fear of man's opinion), rejection, fear of the unknown, fear of death, fear of failure and fear of not being enough. It has many symptoms. Some of the most common are anxiety, depression, insecurity and panic. Doubt and unbelief are even symptoms of fear. Why? Because to doubt God is to question His Word and His authority. Why would we doubt a God whose plans are to prosper us, giving us hope and a future (Jeremiah 29:11)? I will tell you why: fear.

Does this sound familiar? God is wanting to awaken within us a heart that can spot fear from a mile away and face it with truth. Denial will only be a stumbling block to your freedom. If you relate to these signs and symptoms of fear, take heart. God made you with a courageous heart, like David's. He made you for a life of freedom, and He has already given you the weapons you will need to take down this giant and live without fear.

Before we get there, however, it is important to expose fear's plan. Bringing it into the light. When we do this, we stop fear from getting the upper hand. Because when we face fear, we discover something so powerful it begins to shift our perspective from fearful to hopeful.

Fear's Plan Exposed

When the Israelite army first met Goliath at the battle line, the giant Philistine warrior presented himself as indestructible. Everything about him was intimidating. For starters, he stood over nine feet tall, and heavy bronze armor covered him from head to toe. Imagine the size of his javelin and spear. What a daunting sight to see. And then he spoke. His taunting voice boomed through the valley, amplified by the landscape. Each phrase bounced and echoed from side to side between the mountains. There was no escaping it. The seed of fear deposited deep within the hearts of the soldiers grew and grew, consuming their minds and overshadowing their faith. They lost their courage, and with it, they lost sight of the God who promised to fight for them. Their gaze shifted from the Source of their salvation to the object of their fear.

This is fear's textbook strategy. Thousands of years ago and today, it makes its attack in four phases. First, it intimidates us. Second, it amplifies the sound of its deception. Third, it consumes our thoughts and hijacks our body's defense mechanisms. Finally, it seeks to redirect our gaze from the truth, from our Savior, to our circumstances. If fear succeeds, it can paralyze us and render us totally ineffective for the Kingdom of God.

Fear Intimidates

There is a reason the Philistine army chose to send Goliath out before their troops to mock and taunt Israel's army rather than engage them in battle. They knew that one look at him could strike fear in the bravest warrior. Everything about him was intimidating: his size, his armor, his haughty confidence and even his booming voice. It is no surprise he greeted them this way:

Goliath stood and shouted to the ranks of Israel, "Why do you come out and line up for battle? Am I not a Philistine, and are you not the servants of Saul? Choose a man and have him come down to me. If he is able to fight and kill me, we will become your subjects; but if I overcome him and kill him, you will become our subjects and serve us."

1 Samuel 17:8–9

In other words, "Why bother fighting me? Have you seen me? You're not strong enough to defeat me. There's nothing you can do. Your leader is an ordinary man. There is no hope for you." What a bully.

And like a schoolyard bully, fear intimidates us, stripping us of our confidence and determination and rendering us timid and unsure of our strength. If it succeeds, it can even call into question our very identity. That is why Goliath referred to the Israelites as "servants of Saul" instead of acknowledging them as the army of the Lord. First he towered over them physically, and then he called into question their position, power and authority, provoking them to become timid, lacking in courage, doubting who they were and whose army they were fighting for. For all except David, the crippling effect of this intimidation was nearly immediate. Can you relate? I sure can.

Fear Amplifies Its Sound

Have you ever been to the mountains and heard how the sound carries? Instinctively, people will shout or sing loudly just to hear how far their voice will carry and how long it will take for it to bounce back. It is fascinating to experience how sound reverberates off the rocky terrain, causing our voice to echo.

This was the very nature of the landscape on which the Israelites and Philistines faced off. The battle lines were drawn within the Valley of Elah. On either side of the valley were mountains, and running through the center was a river.

Goliath, being the experienced warrior that he was, used the landscape as one gigantic megaphone to intensify and increase the chilling sound of his rebellious and intimidating shouts.

Can you imagine? Twice a day for forty days, some giant more than twice your size shouts threats at you relentlessly—threats that are bounced back and forth multiple times across the terrain. "This day I defy you. . ." Over and over again it comes, like waves crashing on a shore. Before long, the sound of his voice echoes in your mind and torments your heart.

Who would dare fight? The army was losing the battle from the inside out, and who could blame them?

Fear takes what could be simple, meaningless words, thoughts or ideas and amplifies them into a roar, striking hopelessness in our hearts. Before we know it, our fear becomes louder than our faith, shattering our trust and undermining our resolve. If we do not deal with fear at this level, we risk becoming consumed by it.

Fear Consumes

One shout from fear can echo in our minds for days, weeks, months or even years. It is not that we are okay with it nagging relentlessly at our thoughts but rather that we do not know how to deal with it. At some point we become convinced that we will always be afraid. We accept the deafening sound of fear's amplified shouts as a sort of anthem.

When this happens, we cannot help but allow fear to define our steps and consume our thought life, and when it does, we become stuck, paralyzed by fear and utterly unable to move forward. The giant of fear hijacks the narrative of our destiny, a destiny only God Himself should author.

The army of the Lord found themselves in this position. They were consumed by fear. Though they fought no real battle in the valley, their minds were losing a war with fear. They had no idea how to gain the upper hand. They seemed to have accepted their fate: defeat.

Fear Redirects

This is when fear strikes its lethal blow: redirecting our focus from Jesus to our circumstance. Moving us away from truth, fear takes us down a path of distortion and false realities that cements its control over our lives.

In the story of Peter walking on water, the treacherous weather conditions are much more than a rhetorical device to stir up a sense of drama. As the disciples sailed farther out from land, the wind began to pick up, and the waves violently crashed up against their boat. The sound of the storm was no doubt deafening, and I am sure they could think of nothing except for the danger they faced there on the tumultuous waters.

Suddenly, they began to see someone walking toward them on the water. Not realizing it was Jesus, they were terrified, thinking it was a ghost. Instead, "Jesus immediately said to them: 'Take courage! It is I. Don't be afraid'" (Matthew 14:27). It is wild to me that in this moment of intense chaos and fear, Peter decided that to validate Jesus' identity, he would ask Jesus to call him out on the water with Him.

> "Lord, if it's you," Peter replied, "tell me to come to you on the water." "Come," he said. Then Peter got down out of the boat, walked on the water and came toward Jesus.
>
> verses 28–29

With one word from Jesus—"Come"—Peter took a step out onto the water in obedience and walked atop the impossible. In that moment, every limitation and every fear submitted to the authority of Christ, and Peter was carried by the voice of God. Peter's obedience slayed the giant of fear in that moment as he walked forward toward Jesus, atop the impossible. And then Peter noticed the wind. Suddenly, Peter's focus shifted to the elements, and he became afraid. When Peter took his eyes off his Savior and redirected his attention toward the storm, fear trumped Peter's faith, and he began to sink. All the limitations of his flesh came flooding in. Fear created a false reality for Peter that his circumstance controlled his outcome, when really, Jesus had full control over the outcome. After all, it was by Jesus' power that Peter operated without limits to walk on water in the first place. It only took one moment of disbelief for the limitations of Peter's flesh to manifest.

Fear has not picked up any new tricks or strategies over the course of millennia. This is what happened to the Israelites in the valley, and it is also what happens to us today. Now that we know how to anticipate its plan of attack in order to defend ourselves, it is time to start learning how to step up to the battle line and strike back.

Know this: God is setting you up my friend. To look fear in the eye. And when you do, what you will see peering at you from behind its heavy armor is sheer terror. Terror that you, a son or daughter of God, is about to release your roar of breakthrough and charge over that battle line in victory once and for all!

───────────────── **DECLARE IT** //////////////

I will not allow fear to intimidate me, consume me or direct my steps any longer. God controls the outcome, not my circumstances. I am a champion in Christ!

3

The Battle Line
of Breakthrough

For God has not given us a spirit of fear, but of
power and of love and of a sound mind.

2 Timothy 1:7 NKJV

No matter where we are in our journey, we can count
on fear showing up and doing its best to intimidate
and enslave us. It is simply a fact of life that if we
are fulfilling our Kingdom assignments, we will face fears
all the time. Paul said, "For your sake we face death all day
long; we are considered as sheep to be slaughtered" (Romans
8:36). The goal, then, is not so much the absence of fear but
rather successfully holding fast to the presence of God while
we keep going, while we run and do not stop.

My friend, we cannot do that until we come to see fear for
what it is: a predator seeking to demobilize us from obeying

the "go" of the Gospel, which is the last command of Jesus before He ascended into heaven: "Go into all the world and preach the gospel" (Mark 16:15). If we are demobilized, then we are unable to fulfill what God has called us to on this earth.

You do not have to allow fear to take you prisoner and make you its slave. You were created to cry out with a roar of breakthrough at that ugly giant standing at the battle line of your breakthrough. You were created to defeat him, to march boldly past him across the battle line and to enter into the land of God's promise and destiny for your life. Will you dare face the giant and cross confidently over to the land God is calling you to?

Jehovah-Sabaoth, Lord of Armies

Every battle is marked with a line, some sort of intangible division between the two sides. The story of David and Goliath is no exception. The battle began along a dividing line nestled in the Valley of Elah. At the base of the mountain on one side of the valley was the Philistine army, and on the other lay the army of the Lord. Somewhere in the middle, the battle line was drawn. Neither army could cross over to the other side until achieving victory.

Now, if the Israelites had been in their right mind, there would not have been any question which army would win. Time and time again, they had seen God fulfill His promise that He would never leave them or forsake them. In every other battle, the Lord fought for and through them. They had defeated the Philistines every time they fought in the past. So why did this battle cause such an identity crisis?

Along the way, the Israelites forgot whom they really served, and this shift in perspective changed everything. As long as we know God as our Jehovah-Sabaoth, the Lord of Hosts who fights for us, we need never be afraid. When we begin to follow other leaders, however, and remove ourselves from the secure protection of the God of our salvation, fear can quickly get the upper hand. This is what happened in the Valley of Elah.

The Israelites walked up to the battle line with their king, Saul. He was the king they had asked God for (1 Samuel 8:5). He was their leader, their chosen shepherd. It is no surprise that Goliath began his verbal assault by attacking the king. He knew if he could take down the king, the whole army would follow. Remember this passage from earlier?

> Goliath stood and shouted to the ranks of Israel, "Why do you come out and line up for battle? Am I not a Philistine, and are you not the servants of Saul? Choose a man and have him come down to me. If he is able to fight and kill me, we will become your subjects; but if I overcome him and kill him, you will become our subjects and serve us."
>
> 1 Samuel 17:8–9

I can see Goliath shifting his gaze from the army to the king as he said those words: "Aren't you servants of Saul?" I picture him looking down his nose and giving Saul the once-over like, "Yeah, you don't scare me. You're just a man. What can you do?" Everyone in that valley knew that on his own effort, Saul could not do a thing to defend his people against the giant. Goliath's trick worked. He had successfully convinced the army that their sense of safety was all a façade.

It makes me think of the time in the New Testament when the disciples were attempting to cast a demon out of someone. Instead of trusting in Jesus, they tried to invoke the name of "the Jesus whom Paul preaches" (Acts 19:13), like, "You know, that guy Paul talks about who did all the miracles? Him! He'll get you!" Yet, the demon looked them over and said, "Jesus I know, and Paul I know about, but who are you?" (verse 15). Then he "overpowered them" and chased them out of the place "naked and bleeding" (verse 16). They did not stand confidently in their identity as followers of Christ; instead, they just tried to do what they had heard their teacher Paul do. They trusted in him rather than trusting directly in Jesus for themselves.

The enemy knows that the people of God have no real reason to fear, so when he sees an opportunity to shift your focus from your Protector to a person, he will take it. These are battle line moments in our lives. They offer us an opportunity either to partner with our flesh and flee in fear or partner with the Spirit of the living God inside us, who makes us victorious in battle. Scripture tells us, "'Not by might nor by power, but by my Spirit,' says the LORD Almighty" (Zechariah 4:6). When we are toe-to-toe with our own Goliath, that is when we need to remember most that the battle is not ours but the Lord's, and He never loses.

David knew God, not Saul, was his defender, and he knew that God assured His people the victory. The giant had undermined the identity and withered the hearts of every other man in the Israelite ranks, but not David. He approached the battle confident that whatever lies Goliath spewed, his brothers were already the victorious soldiers of Jehovah-Sabaoth. He was so confident, in fact, that he took off running toward Goliath and the battle line as he declared, "You come against me with sword and spear and javelin, but I come against you in the name of the LORD Almighty, the God of the armies of Israel, whom you have defied" (1 Samuel 17:45).

The Hebrew word for "Almighty" in this passage is *tsaba*, which means "army, warfare."* It is here where David calls God Jehovah-Sabaoth, the God of Armies. He was very aware he was a part of the army of the Lord. David raised the name of Jehovah-Sabaoth like a sword to strike fear in the heart of this defiling Philistine giant.

You and I can use this name of God in our everyday battles. When the enemy is coming against our family, our work, our mind and our relationships, we can, like David, run up to the battle line and confidently declare, "You may come at me with all your lies and threats and fear, but today I come at you in the name of Jehovah-Sabaoth. This day I will not bow to fear. I will roar with a roar of breakthrough!" If all it took to silence Israel's most fearsome foe was a shepherd boy who trusted his God, think of what you can do against the giant of fear in your own life—you, a son or daughter of the living God, co-heir with Christ. All you have to do is keep your focus fixed on the Lord of armies, the one who fights for you and has already secured you the victory.

My Battle Line Moment

I will never forget the moment the Lord began to birth this message of slaying the giant of fear in my spirit. It was in the months prior to signing my first book deal. I had submitted my book proposal to two different publishers some months before, but I still had yet to hear if anyone wanted to publish it. The wait was challenging. I was 34 years old at the time, which meant it had been 17 years since the Lord spoke to me very clearly to say, "You will write a book for

*Biblehub.com, s.v. "*tsaba*."

your generation." In that hard season of waiting, God was up to some big things, and it all began to unfold as a result of a Facebook post, of all things.

Before I jump in, let me provide a little context. Though I had experienced significant breakthrough from the debilitating effects of fear and rejection, I continued to struggle on and off, particularly with the fear of conflict and confrontation and that my voice was too small to make any real difference. The enemy knew that—not to mention just how vulnerable I was while I was waiting to hear if my book would be picked up by a publisher—and he did not miss the opportunity to prey on me in this pivotal season in my journey toward the promise of God.

God knew it too, and unbeknownst to me, He had been preparing me for the battle ahead. The Sunday before The Great Facebook Post Saga I found myself utterly captivated and emboldened by the Spirit of the Lord. As I sat in the pew listening to the pastor speaking, the Holy Spirit roared inside me, saying, "Krissy, it's time to rise." I ran to the altar, as He repeated it over and over again. "Krissy, it's time to rise." It felt like a clarion call to shake off the bonds of insecurity and timidity that had been holding me back.

After that, I imagine the enemy could barely wait to get me chained up again. He only waited two or three days before he began his onslaught. Like something out of a movie, it was gloomy, overcast and bitterly cold. I was reading through a magazine when I ran across something that deeply troubled me. I felt the fire of God surge through my bones, as He had at church. *Krissy, it's time to rise.* I thought perhaps this was an opportunity the Lord was highlighting for me, one in which I needed to take a stand boldly for truth, and all I knew was I had given Him my yes. I was nervous about rocking the boat, but I felt confident I was being called to raise my voice for such a time as this, even if it meant challenging others' ideas and ruffling some feathers. I went to social media to share my thoughts on the disturbing article, shaky but emboldened that I was in lockstep with the Spirit.

Later that day my husband and I were out with our kids at a movie theater getting ready to watch the newest children's movie. As we waited for the movie to start, I made the mistake of opening Facebook to check the comments that had come in from my post. And there it was—the opposition that I feared. That *one* person who thought what I was taking a stand for was frivolous. It was not so much the 2.4 *billion* Facebook users that I feared most, but rather the one or two people close to home who might take a stand against me and my stand. And it sure did not take long for the naysayers to emerge. This was just the sort of thing that would shut me down in the past due to my fear of conflict and confrontation, and this day, sadly, was no different.

The battle line in my war with fear had been redrawn, and I did not even realize it. I did my best to tune out the giant of fear so I could enjoy my time at the movies with my family, but I was deeply shaken. I spent the rest of the day trying to rest, recuperate, listen and, above all, discern the voice of God, but fear still managed to intimidate and consume me.

I totally shut down, and I am talking fast! Someone had stood against me, and instead of me rising as God had instructed me to do, I immediately folded. I wanted to curl up in a ball and hide—from Facebook, from publishers, from any and everybody. I wished I had never raised my voice, unaware that what I was really wishing was that I had never given God my big, bold yes to be the voice He was calling me to be.

But here is the beautiful thing about the Lord: He works all things together for His good, and this was no exception. Right there, during that trial, as I cowered and ran from the battle line where fear stood mocking me, the Lord planted a seed. He began to unfold the story of David and Goliath to me supernaturally—this very story about overcoming the giant of fear—and it rocked my world. It was two years before I would write the story of how I slayed my Goliath and crossed over the battle line of my destiny, but let me tell you, it was worth every tear and halting step it took to get there. It is the reason you are holding this book in your hands.

God told me years ago that I would write a book for my generation, and I did. Now I am writing another one and plan to write many, many more. It never would have been written if I had not made that Facebook post in obedience, if that person had not commented on it and if I had not clung to God in desperation to keep from being decimated by fear.

The Battle Line Is Your Point of Breakthrough

Fear always stands where we are made to go. It will always position itself right at the line of our crossing over into the new, into our destiny, into the promise. When you see the giant of fear taking his stand, you can know you are at a pivotal destiny moment. His very presence is an indication you are on the verge of some kind of breakthrough.

But there is something else you need to know: The battle line in front of you is not meant to prevent you from crossing over. It is the line you are authorized by the Lord of Hosts, the God of armies, to draw in the ground to tell your enemy, "You have come far enough. Now your time is done, and mine is beginning."

The Bible says that after David cut off the head of Goliath the army "surged forward" (1 Samuel 17:52) across the battle line to lay hold of their victory. The battle line was not meant to be a stopping point but rather a point of victory. It was their new starting line. The same proved true for me those years ago as I began to understand what God meant when He told me, "Rise."

Right now I want you to take a moment and ask God what His plan is for you. Listen closely for His response. Now look inside your heart and ask yourself what has been holding you back from stepping into that plan. What are you running away from that you sense God may want you to face? Are you stuck? Hesitant? Hindered? What is making you afraid?

When you have identified the answers to these questions, I want you to imagine yourself drawing a line that the enemy cannot cross. As you begin to learn about the three supernatural weapons you possess to slay the giant of fear, my prayer is that you will trust more and more deeply that God has given you the authority to set up your own prophetic boundary line for fear. That line you draw in the Spirit, telling the enemy, "No further." Soon, you will be surging forward, pulling out your first weapon and launching it right at the head of that ugly giant standing in the way of your destiny.

DECLARE IT

When I find I am facing the giant of fear I will rejoice, knowing my breakthrough is near. I am a champion in Christ!

PART 2

Weapon #1
OBEDIENCE

4

Why Obedience?

> But Samuel replied: "Does the LORD delight in
> burnt offerings and sacrifices as much as in obey-
> ing the LORD? *To obey is better than sacrifice*,
> and to heed is better than the fat of rams."
>
> 1 Samuel 15:22, emphasis added

I felt like I was on a treasure hunt, and the Word of God was my map. Each Scripture brought a new level of understanding as I discovered what had been hidden in plain sight all along. Several months into the adventure with the Lord, I was still discovering truths about why obedience is a weapon to slay the giant of fear. I was mining the stories hidden in plain sight throughout the Word of God and learning how others in the Word had wielded obedience as a weapon at their own giant of fear. It was a joy-filled experience, especially after walking through so much fear in the years prior.

I could not wait to bring new questions to the Lord. Early on I found myself scratching my head a bit and wondering,

"Okay, God. But how are these weapons? And why?" Maybe you are also wondering right now why and how something as simple as obedience is a weapon against fear.

Simply put, obedience is doing what is right without fear of the outcome. I discovered that it triggers, activates and puts legs to our faith. Our choice to submit our hearts to the authority and command of our heavenly Father is a love offering to Jesus. When we follow up on that heart posture with steps of obedience, that is, doing what God tells us to do regardless of our fleshly desires, that is an act of faith. And as we will see in the life of David, acts of faith-filled obedience are powerful against the enemy.

Even in the Small Things

What did Jesus say was the greatest of all the commandments? That's right: to love the Lord your God with all your heart, mind, soul and strength (Luke 10:27). But He also said this: "If you love me, obey my commandments" (John 14:15 NLT). If obedience is a demonstration of love, no wonder God called David a man after His own heart. David's life is a picture of obedience. Before he had the chance to be obedient to God's big requests, he demonstrated consistent obedience to the small things.

At a very young age David could be found out in the field tending the sheep. This was not a glamorous job. It meant feeding the lambs and cleaning up their waste. But David was a shepherd, and he knew what it meant to care for a flock.

It is not surprising, then, that when David's dad, Jesse, asked him to bring food to his brothers on the battlefield, David was quick to comply.

> Now Jesse said to his son David, "Take this ephah of roasted grain and these ten loaves of bread for your brothers and hurry to their camp. Take along these ten cheeses to the commander of their unit. See how your brothers are and bring back some assurance from them. They are with Saul and all the men of Israel in the Valley of Elah, fighting against the Philistines."
>
> 1 Samuel 17:17–19

David was compliant and submissive even to his earthly father, including when it meant carrying out small tasks, like bringing food to his brothers and news to his father. He even took the time to leave his sheep with another shepherd to ensure they were cared for while he was away.

It is important to mention here that at this point, David had already been anointed king of Israel. (See 1 Samuel 16.) Yet, he was still serving his family by tending to the sheep. He was still willing to run errands for his dad. He was tall, strong, filled "powerfully" with the Holy Spirit (1 Samuel 16:13) and fully able to fight in battle, but because his father did not send him to the battle lines, he remained obediently at home, serving his family.

How many of us would respond as David did on the heels of such a moment of anointing? Often when God does something we expect Him to transition us immediately into that new territory. But this is not how God works. Our obedience in the small things positions us for the bigger picture. All the while, God is working through process, through steps and transitions. He is always moving, but His pace is much different than ours. Because of that, obedience can look more like waiting than charging forward.

Often this is what we fear most, staying in the same place for too long. We worry we will never be moved out of the field when we are anointed for the palace, but our pace is based on our limited, carnal view and can be very narrow. Everything God does, on the other hand, is driven by eternity. His vantage point is not limited to our earthly measurement of time. He is an eternal God with an eternal view. So when He calls us He has a season of preparing us, and how long that season will last is totally up to Him.

We need to keep in mind that His calling includes our preparation. Even Jesus had a season of preparation, thirty years, to be precise. Jesus spent three decades living among the sheep, shepherding from afar and learning the hearts of men from a unique vantage point. It was all purposeful, if not particularly glamorous.

We need not fear the small steps because they lack the luster we are after. God needs our compliance to His leading to get us where we need to be. David feared God and was the man for the job of leading His people well. If we will follow his example and posture ourselves after God's heart, we will discover a wild adventure we never could have imagined.

Hardwired for Obedience

I wonder sometimes if David sensed the adventure that was unfolding before him as he stepped up to the battlegrounds. Or was it, in the moment, just chaos?

> David left his things with the keeper of supplies, ran to the battle lines and asked his brothers how they were. As he was talking with them, Goliath, the Philistine champion from Gath, stepped out from his lines and shouted his usual defiance, and David heard it. Whenever the Israelites saw the man, they all fled from him in great fear.
>
> 1 Samuel 17:22–24

As we have discussed, David was outraged at the giant's heresy and shocked to find the Israelites in such distress. An army who has seen the hand of God rescue them time and again was shut down and paralyzed by fear. His countrymen were shattered from within, terrorized by one monstrous giant shouting at them from the battle line. Disgusted, David asked the question, "Who is this uncircumcised Philistine that he should defy the armies of the living God?" (verse 26).

Here is the thing about David: He loved the Lord, and he feared God, not man. Because of that love, David was hardwired toward obedience. He was predisposed to comply with God's commands. Showing up on the field that day triggered his fear and love of the Lord to stir deeply within him.

Remember, Jesus revealed in John 14:15 that the key to obedience is loving Him. The Passion Translation puts it this way: "Loving me *empowers* you to obey my commands" (emphasis added). David was not privy to the teachings of Jesus to be able to make the connection. He was simply living out this truth. David was supernaturally empowered to obey the Lord because of His deep love for God, and hearing Goliath shouting and defiling the name of the Lord catapulted him to action.

It was not even that God told David to go fight Goliath. David was simply doing what was right without worrying about the outcome, like a reflex. When we love God, our heart desires and His become one. We can step into a situation and approach it the way God would because we are connected to His heart. We fear not because our obedience positions us to ignore the giant of fear. We hear him less and less when we are focused on our Father's business. Fear will continue to shout, but his clamor becomes white noise we can tune out.

Many want to categorize obedience as legalistic, but David's life demonstrates that it is anything but. Obedience rooted in love is a powerful weapon. It is part of an incredible cycle—love leads to obedience, and loving God is our greatest mandate. This deepens our love for and awe of God, which brings us closer and closer to the heart of the Father, as well as to new levels of victory over the battles in our lives. Why? Because the more we love, know and trust God experientially, the more we understand the outcome is the Lord's. And so is the battle. God's words to Judah and Jerusalem so many millennia ago are no less encouraging for us today: "Do not be afraid or discouraged because of this vast army. For the battle is not yours, but God's" (2 Chronicles 20:15).

Obedience Gives Us New Perspective

Walking in obedience does not just mean following God's step-by-step instructions for our life. That is a big part of it, yes, but walking in obedience is essentially our agreement with God's heart for us. It is our compliance with His nature and will for the earth.

The Bible states the earth and everything in it is the Lord's. David wrote these words in the Psalms to describe what he understood of God: "The earth is the LORD's, and everything in it, the world, and all who live in it; for he founded it on the seas and established it on the waters" (Psalm 24:1–2). Our obedience to Him, or our agreement with His laws and instructions for life on this planet, becomes a by-product of our alignment with His heart.

God wants to align our perspective with His so that when fear comes a-knocking, we answer the door. This is something a friend of mine, Abigail Holt-Jennings, said when she was faced with a terminal diagnosis of breast cancer. She told me she wanted to cower in fear at the sound of that diagnosis, but the roar of breakthrough rose up from within her and shifted her perspective. Instead of running in fear, she looked it in the eye and said, "Not today!" Miraculously, she was totally healed of stage-four breast cancer.*

So often we fear admitting we are afraid. We think we have to put on a bold front all the time, especially in the Christian community, right? We tell ourselves, "If I am afraid, then what kind of faith do I have? If the Bible says, 'Faith the size of a mustard seed can move mountains,' and I am over here trembling in fear, then I must not even have a smidgen of faith."

Baloney!

Do not buy into this. In fact, let's break agreement right here, right now with that lie that says, "If I fear, then I don't have faith." It is when we begin to allow ourselves to feel what we feel that we can begin to address it, move on and shift our perspective. If we do not do this, we risk becoming self-dependent instead of Jesus-dependent. And friend, we need Jesus.

Acknowledging our limitations and weakness in the natural makes room for the supernatural. Remember what Paul said:

> But he said to me, "My grace is sufficient for you, for my power is made perfect in weakness." Therefore I will boast all the more gladly about my weaknesses, so that Christ's power may rest on me.
>
> 2 Corinthians 12:9

*You can read more about her story in her book *The Conversation in Heaven.*

This is really good news!

The truth is, you are human, and as such, fear is normal. Most of the time our flesh wants to flee in fear, right? I mean, let's be real here. I am over here raising my own hand as I write. Since you are reading this book, I know you understand this, too. It does not make sense to fear being afraid because it might mean you do not have faith. Rather, admit like Paul, "I am weak. I am afraid here. But I know who is greater. I know who is stronger." This perspective allows me to come to the conclusion that my very real fear is actually irrelevant, because greater is He who is in me, than he who is in the world (1 John 4:4). I can then look fear in the eye, knowing it is an empty threat compared to the promises of God.

Facing fear feels unnatural or wrong because looking fear in the eye is not something we do naturally. It is, however, something we do supernaturally, by the Spirit—the same Spirit "who raised Christ from the dead" (Romans 8:11). Even when we are so paralyzed with fear that we do not think we will make it out alive, we can be confident in God's promise of resurrection power within, that His Spirit will "give life to [our] mortal bodies."

So do not be afraid of being afraid. Admitting you feel fear is key in defeating the giant of fear. The enemy does not want you admitting when you feel afraid; he just wants you reacting to fear and fleeing the scene, because when you flee, you cannot cross over into the land of your victory.

If the Israelite army had been able to stop and say, "That giant is scary, yes, but my God is bigger," they could have been victorious immediately. Instead, they tucked their tails between their legs and ran off terrified. David, on the other hand, saw the same giant. He heard the same giant. But he did not act in fear, not even for a second. Why? Because he was so connected to God that his spirit's desire to obey trumped his fleshly instinct to fear. David feared the Lord more than Goliath, and his concern was what might happen if this giant who was mocking the army of the Lord was not dealt with, and swiftly.

David's obedience to honor the heart of God took the form of a simple stone pulled from a stream and launched into the face of the giant. His alignment with God's heart gave him a right perspective that we are all meant to have. It gave him victory over fear, and over his fearsome enemy.

Empowered to Obey

> There is no fear in love. But perfect love drives out fear, because fear has to do with punishment. The one who fears is not made perfect in love.
>
> 1 John 4:18

Obedience is not just about rules and precepts. Yes, He longs that we follow His precepts for our lives. But not outside of fellowship with Him. Jesus calls His disciples to "Come follow Me." He says, "If you love Me, you'll obey My commands" (John 14:15). In fact—even better—"Loving me empowers you to obey my commands" (TPT). This is God's desire for us. The longing of His heart is for us to know Him and grow in love for Him to such a degree that, like David, we cannot help but obey because His desires are our desires. He does not ever want us to be more focused on the "doing" than we are on Him.

This relationship does not mean you will not feel fear. Believe me, you will know when you are toe to toe with that enemy. But from now on, you will feel the weapon of obedience in your hand, and you will be able to use it effectively against the giant before his tactics of intimidation can begin to impact your faith. You will sense God's love surrounding you like a shield, driving out fear and bringing peace to your heart. Free of fear's choke hold around your neck, you will be able to take a deep breath—and take down that giant!

DECLARE IT

I will dare to look fear in the eye and declare its fate. Fear has no power or hold on my life. I am a champion in Christ!

5

Postured for Victory

"I have told you these things, so that in me you
may have peace. In this world you will have trouble. But take heart! I have overcome the world."

John 16:33

As you may have realized by now, this book is not a
quick fix for us to slap away fear and win the battle
overnight. But the good news—and it is really, really
good news—is that God designed a solution to overcoming
fear that is even better than a Band-Aid. Instead of an external
remedy we can apply and then remove, or let fall off, this victory is something that begins deep within us. From the inside
out, we slay the giant of fear in every area of our lives as our
perspective shifts and we take on a new posture that makes us
resistant to the intimidating, loud, once all-consuming effect
of the giant's cries. But like most things in the Kingdom of
God, that posture may not be what you expect.

Obedience Gives Us a New Posture

Bold, grandiose, confident actions can be both godly and very effective against the enemy. But over the course of our battle against the giant of fear, the seemingly small steps toward victory are often most significant. We must stop overlooking the power of consistent, minor shifts in our posture, perspective and behavior to instead focus on what we assume are taller stepping stones to the "big thing." We must realize, "Oh, these *are* the big things!"

If you have walked with the Lord for any length of time, you have probably noticed that God likes to do the unexpected:

When I am weak, then I am strong.

2 Corinthians 12:10

Blessed are the meek, for they will inherit the earth.

Matthew 5:5

God chose the foolish things of the world to shame the wise; God chose the weak things of the world to shame the strong.

1 Corinthians 1:27

So it should be no surprise that when it comes to overcoming fear, the best posture for us to take is not one of prideful confidence in our victory but of humility and submission to the Lord. This does not mean God wants us to be wimpy. It means that when we humble ourselves before God and His will for our lives and actions, He will raise us up; we do not have to do it ourselves. It means that when we take a posture of submission to Him, we can be at peace, even in the midst of the storm.

Look at David. Look at the posture he walked in. David certainly was not wimpy. We always think of him as bold and courageous, but he was also meek and submitted to the godly and earthly authority over his life. That is why he is a representation of the spirit. Remember Elijah's encounter with the Spirit of the Lord?

> The Lord said, "Go out and stand on the mountain in the presence of the LORD, for the LORD is about to pass by." Then a great and powerful wind tore the mountains apart and shattered the rocks before the LORD, but the LORD was not in the wind. After the wind there was an earthquake, but the LORD was not in the earthquake. After the earthquake came a fire, but the LORD was not in the fire. And after the fire came a gentle whisper. . . . "What are you doing here, Elijah?"
>
> 1 Kings 19:11–13

Does the Lord have the power to move mountains, shake the earth and burn like a flame? Yes. But His whisper is no less mighty.

David stepped into chaos and maintained his peace from the time he entered the valley to the moment he cut off the giant's head. Ultimately, it was not the throw that brought Goliath down. No, he defeated him in the name of Jehovah-Sabaoth through the courage he carried in his heart. That courage caused him to take one step after the other, asking questions to collect information, and approaching Saul to gain permission to take on the giant himself. It was the reason he rejected Saul's armor after trying it on. It compelled him to pick up no more than five small stones, put them in his pouch and then run toward the fearsome giant, slaying him for good. One small, obedient step after the other led an entire army in victory.

David did not react to fear. He responded to it, filtering it through what He knew of God. It is what gave him the boldness to run toward Goliath unafraid. It was what gave David the power to defeat him. If this inspires you, imagine what it did for the Israelite army. David's posture of submissive obedience made a pathway of courage that allowed the entire army to "surge forward" (1 Samuel 17:52). God had gone before them through one meek-yet-strong vessel, David, a shepherd boy, and that knowledge put the shattered pieces of their bravery back together.

Trust Matters

David's son, Solomon, was perhaps the wisest man who had ever lived. In that wisdom, he wrote this admonition: "Trust in the Lord with all your heart, and lean not on your own understanding; in all your ways acknowledge Him, and He shall direct your paths" (Proverbs 3:5–6 NKJV). Humility and submission to authority require trust. You cannot assume the posture of obedience without it.

Look at the story of Mary, whom God chose to bear His Son on the earth. The angel greeted her and referred to her as "highly favored" (Luke 1:28). He then informed her she was chosen by God to carry His Son. Her response to this news should light a fire in us: "'I am the Lord's servant,' Mary answered. 'May your word to me be fulfilled'" (Luke 1:38). Instead of arguing or giving in to any fear of the impossible that she may have felt, she came into agreement with God's heart for her and simply complied. She humbly chose to trust the Lord and posture herself as a willing vessel instead of giving in to fear—fear of the unknown, fear of man, etc.

This kind of trust requires relationship. Mary knew God intimately. She trusted Him because she knew He was trustworthy. The same is true of David's walk with the Lord. The pattern is always the same: Love leads to obedience. Obedience builds trust. Trust creates an atmosphere in which submission can flourish. A life of humble submission to God leads to triumph over fear.

God is looking for a people who will posture themselves before Him as willing vessels that He might use in miraculous ways to bring glory to His name. Instead of us fearing the unknown and what may or may not happen, or fearing that we might mess it up, or fearing what others might think, we can take a page out of Mary's book and simply show up with our yes, saying, "Okay, Lord, be it unto me as You will. I am but your servant." This is obedience. And it closes the door to fear.

How can fear take a stand in our lives when we are standing on our Rock, deeply rooted and in love with our King? A posture of humility allows God to work through us and annihilate this giant because our focus is not on fear; it is on Jesus. As we form a supernatural habit of obeying His voice instead of the voice of fear, we become Spirit-based thinkers, like David. With that posture and foundation, anything is possible to you. (See Mark 9:23.)

A Matter of the Mind

Here is the tricky thing: The enemy knows all this. He also knows it is unlikely that he will, with one battle, alter your love for God. So he goes after a more reasonable and likely stepping stone: your trust in God and submission to His plan. His go-to tactic? Intimidation.

In an earlier chapter we discussed the enemy's agenda with fear: to intimidate, amplify the sound, consume and redirect. This is why intimidation is a main objective of fear. He will do anything and everything he can to bully you into trusting him more than God, because if fear can manage to make you think he is truth, he can undermine your trust in the God of truth.

When this shift happens, instead of a posture of meekness before the Lord, our shoulders sink in timid despair. We become demoralized instead of empowered. And when we are demoralized through intimidation, it is like we become disoriented. Our peaceful clarity about our mission and the victory building inside of us are replaced by bewilderment, and our courage and obedient discipline fly out the window. We pray for quick fixes to end our agony, and we shut down from the inside outward.

Can you see it? This is what Goliath was doing to the army. It is what Satan wants to do to us through fear, because if he can deprive us of our trust in God, our courage and our discipline, and destroy us from within, throwing us into total panic and confusion, we will run away and let him win.

Take a step back for a moment and allow yourself to see the intangible nature of all of this. This is a matter of the mind. That is where the real threat lies. And "we have the mind of Christ" (1 Corinthians 2:16). When our mind is in Christ, the enemy cannot win. As long as we remember this, as long as we take time to remain focused on our God, Jehovah-Sabaoth, Lord of Armies, fear will not be able to intimidate us into backing down. Fear will not be able to shake our trust in God. It will not succeed in getting us to submit to itself instead of the Father.

My friend, do you love God with all your heart, mind, soul and strength? If you can confidently say yes, then good! But

I have another question: If so, why are you giving the voice of the giant access to your thought life? Why are you fleeing in fear before an enemy who has already been defeated by the victory of the cross? If you know "the one who is in you is greater than the one who is in the world" (1 John 4:4–6), what is keeping you from trusting the Lord enough to submit to Him, to admit you are afraid and to step back and allow Jehovah-Sabaoth to fight for you?

I do not say this to bring condemnation. Do not be ashamed. But you must be willing to admit what is going on. You are human, and you are "being transformed into [the image of God] with ever-increasing glory" (2 Corinthians 3:18). So give yourself grace, and embrace the process. You are being trained right now, today as you read this book. God is developing you into who He sees you to be: a champion, a warrior and His bride.

If for any reason you hesitated in saying yes above in confident assurance that you love the Lord with all your heart, mind, soul and strength, then first, let me say I commend you for your honesty. It is not that you are saying no; rather, you are becoming aware that perhaps you have not nurtured your love for the Lord through intimacy with Jesus as you would hope. This is quite normal. In fact, we should always be growing in this area. So, fear not. You are not alone. I want to challenge you today to spend time at the feet of Jesus. The Word promises, "Seek me and [you will] find me when you seek me with all your heart" (Jeremiah 29:11). Seek Him today, my friend, and you will find a passion and fire from deep within you beginning to grow as your love for Christ deepens through greater intimacy.*

*For more resources to help you grow in maturity and intimacy with Christ, visit my website, krissynelson.com.

Trust God with Your Mess

Have you ever walked away from a painful battle, something you thought you overcame, only to discover that the ramifications of that event seem to follow you into your future far longer than you ever imagined? If you are like me, you may find that the lingering effects of that mess are sometimes harder to address than the giant you conquered in your past.

After fighting a giant like fear, you are going to be tired. You are likely going to have wounds. You will be ready to sink back into the loving embrace of the Father and close your eyes to rest and enjoy the security of victory. But sometimes, just as your eyes are nearly shut, you will see the foot soldiers of your fallen enemy are still straggling behind you. Even when the battle is won and the enemy is defeated, it is like a trail of chaos somehow manages to follow you for months and even years after a traumatic event. *Ugh.* Can you relate to this?

I want to encourage you: Do not fear the mess. Often we avoid dealing with things and addressing the mess because we do not want it to get, well, messier. It can be easier to put up with the status quo than to take the time and energy to get free, really free, of a fight that caused us so much pain. But, friend, you and I were made for freedom.

In cases like this, it is our fleshly instinct to moan, throw our hands up in the air and cry, "Why, oh why is this happening to me?" Here is the thing: It is not that God wants us to go through troubles in life; it is just that troubles are inevitable. Even when we are doing things right, there will be messes to clean up. The battlefields in our lives will be littered with debris even after the war is over. That does not mean we should give up. It certainly is not a reason to declare our effort is meaningless and stay out of the fight altogether. Rather, we have the privilege of walking through life tall and confident, accepting that troubles are part of life and knowing we already have the victory because we have Jesus. The pathway of victory has already been blazed before us by Christ, who told us, "In this world you will have trouble. But take heart! I have overcome the world" (John 16:33).

This is where our lifestyle of obedience and submission to the Lord comes into play again. Our knee-jerk reaction should be to go before the Lord and ask Him, "Father, what is the right thing for me to do in this situation? How do You want me to handle this? I will do whatever You say, even if the outcome is messy. I will not fear." We have got to keep it that simple: releasing the outcome to the Lord, posturing ourselves in total surrender and trusting Him to clean up the mess and heal our heart in the process.

Regardless of how it seems, you can take heart, my friend. You can be of good cheer. You can approach your day, your struggles and your messes armed in the full armor of the Lord. Take up the helmet of salvation, the breastplate of righteousness and the belt of truth. Take each step in the peace of God that passes all understanding, because Jesus is already victorious over the giant of fear. The battle will come and go. There will be messes to clean up. And all the while your response can be the same: simply to stand in who you are in God. You can stand in who God is in you.

God Will Go Before You

Peering down at me in the shadows of the dimly lit library stood the figure of someone I feared, the one person, in fact, I had worked so hard to avoid. This was an individual who had stabbed a knife of betrayal deep within my heart. Instead of ignoring me, as I would have hoped, the person walked right up to my table, stared down at me, and unleashed a tirade of disapproval about me and my ministry.

In that moment I had a choice to make: to allow fear to consume me, or rely on Jehovah-Sabaoth to rise within. Miraculously, I felt a supernatural courage that I cannot explain to this day. As much as I wanted to shut down, I reached into my little shepherd's bag and grabbed the stone of obedience. I threw it at that ugly giant of fear and continued forward across the enemy's line right into the new land God had prepared for me. God had my yes, so the right thing for me to do was advance without fear of the outcome, because after all, the battle is the Lord's. He was my defender. He was my deliverer. He was my strong tower and my fortress. Whatever it cost me, my eyes would remain fixed on Him and Him alone. The roar of my breakthrough manifested itself through three simple words: "Have a seat," I said, inviting the person to join me.

I could hardly believe what I had just done. Neither could my flesh. I was face to face with one of the individuals the enemy had used years prior to try to shut me down from the inside out, and I am not going to lie, my flesh was terrified. My flesh wanted to run, hide and curl up in a little ball in my room never to see the light of day again. But in that moment my flesh was not in charge. My spirit was calling the shots.

As the very personification of my fears sat before me, I knew I had a choice to make: yield to fear or honor the Lord through my obedience. I chose the latter, to honor Him in trusting that He had been preparing me for such a time as this, not to drape me in fear but to clothe me in His robe of righteousness as His beloved daughter who was not fighting this battle alone.

I know beyond a shadow of a doubt that God had been preparing me for that moment of opportunity. You see, in the weeks prior the Lord had given me dreams of bumping into the very person I encountered. The dreams included instructions for what I was to say before and during our conversation. When it actually happened, I realized I was ready.

Want to hear something else miraculous? Before our confrontation I was sitting at this table writing. I had literally just put the period on 2 Timothy 1:7 (NKJV)—"For God has not given us a spirit of fear, but of power and of love and of a sound mind"—when I noticed this person standing there. Not only did God prepare me in the form of prophetic dreams, but He also took the time to orchestrate a reminder in the moment that He had empowered me with everything I would need to face this individual.

The outcome of this day was not one of hugs and roses and butterflies. It was messy. It was painful and ugly. It hurt deeply. But I was able to speak truth into all the lies and chaos. I was simply able to speak the truths that the Lord had given me in my dream and nothing more or less, and I ended the confrontation having gained the upper hand over the giant of fear.

To be honest, after that day I wanted to curl up in a ball and hide forever. My flesh wanted to shut down in shock and never be in the spotlight again. But God had other plans. He was calling me to rise, and only out of sheer obedience to the Lord did I continue to advance. I tell you what—this became a divine opportunity for me to experience the powerful weapon of obedience at work. My simple steps forward in faith, launching my TV show when all my flesh wanted to do was hide, slayed the giant of fear and launched me into a life of true freedom, finally, never the same again. This moment, the moment I feared most, became the catalyst to my long-term victory over fear. Hooray!

My friend, you truly can *take heart*—Jesus has overcome the world. Be of good cheer today. What is God calling you to do? Rest assured, whatever it is, God will not send you into battle alone. He will go in before you and prepare the way, and then He will invite you to join Him. When He does, how will you answer?

God is calling His beloved into a season of posturing ourselves as His humble servants. This season is all about making His name known in the earth and bringing glory to His Son. The enemy is terrified that the army of the Lord will advance in simple obedience without fear of outcome. He is shaking in His boots, my friend, and that makes me excited to continue forward, facing my fears and brushing right past them, eyes locked on Jesus. Are you coming with me?

DECLARE IT

I will not shrink back in fear. I will rise in the joy of the Lord. I am a champion in Christ!

6

Because He Said So

For our struggle is not against flesh and blood,
but against the rulers, against the authorities,
against the powers of this dark world and against
the spiritual forces of evil in the heavenly realms.
Therefore put on the full armor of God, so that
when the day of evil comes, you may be able
to stand your ground, and after you have done
everything, to stand.

Ephesians 6:12–13

The battle between Goliath and the army of Israel
is a physical representation of a very real spiritual
battle. That battle occurs every day in the very real
supernatural realm, where angels are warring against the
powers of darkness that would aim to steal, kill and destroy
our future as God's kids. For many believers today, the battle
is not against our flesh, our bodies, but over our soul, our

mind and our destiny—the intangible and most crucial parts of ourselves.

You see, each day we wake up with God's destiny over our lives. The enemy does not want to see God's people advance, so he draws a battle line, sets up camp, and places giants along it, blocking our way into the fullness of God's plans for us. Then he does everything he can to ensure we never cross over it into our breakthrough, our promised land.

As you know all too well, fear is one of the enemy's favorite giants. His goal is to paralyze us with his intimidating voice or, better yet, get us to give up entirely so that we set up camp on the opposite side and just hang tight in that one spot for a long, long time. The enemy would love if we got really cozy in our camp. He would love to see us building houses and businesses right in the place of our stopping, because then we never advance to the new land God is calling us to take.

This is why cultivating a lifestyle of obedience toward God is essential to overcoming this enemy. As we learn to allow our spirit, not our flesh, to dictate how we act and react, we develop a new perspective and a new posture, as we have seen in the last few chapters, but we also gain new priorities—God's priorities.

Look again at David. Instead of seeing a giant he was afraid of, he saw an unauthorized human disgracing the army of the Lord. Instead of cowering in fear, he chose to trust God and submit his life into His hands. Instead of considering the very plausible negative outcomes (in the natural), his priority in that moment was to honor the Lord in making this wrong thing right. Without a second thought he took matters into his own hands.

As David approached Goliath he said to him, "You come against me with sword and spear and javelin, but I come against you in the name of the LORD Almighty, the God of the armies of Israel, whom you have defied" (1 Samuel 17:45). David took his stand in obedience toward the giant. It was not a direct order he received from the Lord, like "Go kill the giant Goliath." It was obedience from the place of knowing God's heart and prioritizing what God wanted over what circumstances were before him. David knew God's heart, so he knew that what God desired for His people, Israel, was to take the land before them and cross over in victory.

He surely knew engaging with Goliath was dangerous. He knew Goliath could kill him. He knew he was not even a soldier in the army and that some of the men might scoff to see him approach the battle line. He knew the safer bet was delivering his brothers' food and returning with news for Jesse. But none of that mattered, because carrying out God's will and honoring His name was at the forefront of David's mind.

Whatever type of fear we may deal with in the spiritual battles of our lives—fear of failure, fear of death, fear of rejection, fear of man—our priority cannot be our comfort. Our priority cannot be self-preservation or acclaim. Our priority cannot be avoiding conflict to maintain the peace. Our priority has to be doing everything we can do to see God's will played out on earth as it is in heaven. That kind of obedience is what catapults you into your destiny.

Because He Says So

If the enemy can exhaust our focus with fear, he can influence our priorities. He will do all he can to cause us to fix our focus on fear instead of on what pleases Jesus, the author and perfector of our faith.

He reminds us how intimidating it can be to face what we cannot control. He whispers scary "What if?" questions about the unknown, the new—even about that land that we long so badly to cross into. If he is successful, before we know it we may even find ourselves fearing our own destiny. Strange, isn't it? Despite the supernatural pull we feel to cross into the new things God has prepared for us, we wait, toe-to-toe with fear, camped out on the wrong side of the valley.

Have you heard those "What ifs?" before? They usually go something like this:

- What if I'm not really ready to live in the promised land?
- What if it requires more from me than I can give?
- What if I mess up my destiny?
- What if once I'm there, God asks me to do something uncomfortable?

They are valid questions. We are allowed to ask them. But we should not allow them to keep us from our created purpose. A life of obedience to God is the only thing that will set us up to move past these unknowns in order to serve the will of the Father.

Let's face it. You and me, and all the other humans on this planet, are tiptoers. Yes, I may have just made that word up. But think about it for a moment. We like to tiptoe. We want to dip our toe in carefully and test the waters before jumping in, right? That just sounds like good wisdom, does it not? Well, if it was a predator-infested river in Africa, then sure, it is wisdom. But we are talking about the promised land of our destiny. The very land God put us on this planet to occupy. There is no tiptoeing about that; when it comes to our calling and destiny, we can only cannonball.

God is inviting us to step in faith into the unknown, knowing that Jesus is there waiting on the other side with arms open wide, ready for us when we arrive. We simply take the step, and when we do, God parts the waters and shows us the pathway to the promise.

It is just like the people crossing over the Jordan River into the Promised Land. They were instructed to take a step of faith and obedience, and then—only then—the waters would part.

> Now the Jordan is at flood stage all during harvest. Yet as soon as the priests who carried the ark reached the Jordan and their feet touched the water's edge, the water from upstream stopped flowing. It piled up in a heap a great distance away . . . So the people crossed over.
>
> Joshua 3:15–16

We have to step into the unknown to see breakthrough. We have to go in obedience, and as we do, we will slay the giant of fear with each step forward in faith.

It is your time to embrace where God is calling you and simply go. Why? Because He said so. Period. You may have to go without understanding. You may have to start the journey without a roadmap. But that kind of obedience to God's plan and priorities is the mandate of heaven for the people of God. "Without faith it is impossible to please God" (Hebrews 11:6). We are created to trust Him with abandon and to walk in step with the Holy Spirit. You were created for this, even if it does not yet feel like it.

Why Me, God?

Several years ago when I was working on my first book, *Created for the Impossible*, I suffered from major impostor syndrome, or what I like to call the "Why me?" epidemic. You know what I am talking about. It is when you start to walk in obedience to the call of God, maybe even on the other side of the battle line, and you find yourself praying over and over, "Well, God, here we are, walking out this promise together. But now that You have brought me here, I don't understand why You would choose me to do this thing. Why *me*?" Your priorities are focused on God's will, but it just seems unbelievable and maybe impossible that He would ask you to participate in His plan, when others could do it better.

Time and again, I would show up for my day, pen in hand. Okay, it was more like laptop on lap. The point is, I was ready to write. And as I would start, I would often think of all the amazing women of God out there who had tons of influence and could no doubt write this very book way better than I could. Staring at the blank screen before me, I would think "Why me, God? Why do You want *me* to write this when so many others could do it bigger and better than I?"

Do you know what His answer was every time? "Because I said so." Every . . . single . . . time. Eventually I stopped asking the question. I still thought it on occasion, but His answer became so hardwired in my subconscious that I basically began answering the question before I even had the chance to get it out.

Because He said so. That became my *why*. God had called me to write a book, and the point was not that it be some incredible best seller. Yes, that is an awesome goal for any writer. But that could not be my purpose. My objective, my priority, was obedience.

It turned out, that was the antidote to my fears of not being good enough, qualified enough, influential enough, or just plain enough in general. What I was signing up for was not perfection but rather obedience. And if God told me to do it, then who was I to argue with Him?

We look at the life of Jesus, and we see perfectly modeled for us a life aligned with the priorities of heaven. Christ shows us what being "about My Father's business" looks like (Luke 2:49 NKJV) and how it is walked out:

through intimacy with the Father

through fellowship with the saints

through walking into the unknown, the uncharted, the seemingly scary, the "this does not make sense"

Jesus had to face fear, just like we do. The devil sure tried everything at his disposal to bring Jesus down to an earthly point of view and value system, instead of a heavenly one. Just look at that time in the desert. Jesus had been fasting for forty days, and the devil came to him and showed him all the land that he, Satan, could give to Jesus, if only Jesus would bow to him. But Jesus knew "to obey is better than sacrifice" (1 Samuel 15:22). His priority was to do His Father's business.

We bow to the devil when we give in to him by entertaining his lies over God's voice of truth, allowing him to undercut our identity and shift our priorities. It is time for the people of God to stop giving ear to the enemy and his giants and be all-in with the priorities of heaven. Our prayer should be that of Jesus from Matthew 6:10: "Your kingdom come, your will be done, on earth as it is in heaven." When you allow obedience to His call to become your top priority, you are filled with boldness and courage to continue taking those steps forward, even if you are afraid. Even if fear pursues you, you will move forward. Why? Because He said so.

Do Not Get Too Comfortable

My friend, do not prioritize your comfort over obedience to God's call. Do not grow comfortable on the wrong side of the battle line. I will say it another way: Be cautious that you are not mistaking fear for faith and justifying that where you have set up camp is where God wants you to remain.

This can happen subtly if we are not careful. We see the giant of fear. We listen to his taunts, and we allow intimidation to manipulate us into thinking we are meant to just stay right over here on the wrong side of the battle line with all the other soldiers. We tell ourselves our priorities are just fine and that waiting is what would honor God most in the situation. We say, "Oh, I'm just waiting on the Lord. He is calling me to a season of rest right now. I am supposed to hang tight and wait on a word from heaven telling me to advance." How many of us can relate to this? (I am raising my hand!)

Or how about this? "Well, I know God would not want me to strive, so if I try to go any farther I will risk striving for something. When it is God's timing it will just be easy, and then I will walk into the plans He has for my life." Can you relate to that? (Again, I am raising my hand right now.)

Here is something very important we need to remember and be bold enough to embrace about the life of the believer: Jesus did not promise us rainbows and sunshine all the time.

He promised us a combination of beauty and trials. He said, "In this world you will have trouble. But take heart! I have overcome the world" (John 16:33). Serving God is often not following a smooth path. Sometimes it will call us to hard work and sacrifice, or even the death of something we cared deeply for. (See John 12:25.) Obedience is doing it anyway, because it is what He asked us to do—*because God said so.*

As His servants, we know His heart, and we know that His heart and His plan is to use us, His children, His army, as vessels to slay giants and reclaim territory on the earth for the glory of God and the name of Jesus. Whether or not it feels like it, we can withstand anything the enemy would throw at us because we are standing firm in the full armor of God. We will be able to fulfill our destiny in the promised land, regardless of what it demands from us or costs us, because God has called and equipped us to be there. So we stand. And then we advance, even if it takes us the rest of our lives. We do not stop moving forward in obedience. No, instead, we get out our next weapon.

DECLARE IT

I resolve to be okay not having all the answers. I trust the Lord and will advance simply because He is calling me to, because He said so. I am a champion in Christ!

PART 3

Weapon #2
FAITHFULNESS

7

Why Faithfulness?

But the fruit of the Spirit is love, joy, peace, forbearance, kindness, goodness, *faithfulness*, gentleness and self-control.

Galatians 5:22–23, emphasis added

Think about it for a moment: What is fear, really, but an attack on our follow-through? In essence, it is simply an attempt to shut us down so we do give up. Quit. Run the other way. Stop pursuing God's plan.

Faithfulness is a weapon we use against fear because faithfulness is follow-through. It means we keep on going and are faithful to finish what God has called us to. It means we press on. We put our hand to the plow, day-in and day-out. When we are faithful, the enemy cannot intimidate us through fear. Why? Because like obedience, faithfulness fixes our eyes on Jesus.

Faithfulness brings about growth, pulls our roots deep in the Lord and makes us strong. Fear cannot steer the actions of a faithful one because their trust in the Lord runs deep. Their allegiance is to the Lord alone, to the Lamb of God who sits on the throne. As a result, people who are faithful finish what God started in them. They show up. They do not need to be seen, recognized or acknowledged by people. That is because they know that faithfulness is always seen by God, and that is enough.

Faithful ones are captivated by Christ. He has captivated their gaze, and they are caught up in Him, so much so that fear no longer has a voice in their lives. They become firm in adherence to His promises and continue to walk in obedience, full of faith.

Sound like a place you would like to be? Me too. That is because a big part of our life's purpose, why God created man, was so that we would pursue His Son. The passionate pursuit of Christ is hardwired into our being. It is how we were designed to live, declaring with our lives and our loyalty, "I am my beloved's and my beloved is mine" (Song of Solomon 6:3). Like the bride preparing herself for her Bridegroom, our created purpose is to love our God with all our heart, mind, soul and strength as He woos us into deep intimacy with Him.

The more faithful we are to the Lord of our life, the more victorious we will be against the giant of fear in our circumstances. How can fear get a grip on our lives when we are so caught up in loving Christ? When our heart's delight is hearing Him speak to us, leaning our head against His chest and hearing His heart beat, what can fear do? How could it ever move us from this place? It really cannot—unless we allow it to. Fear cannot move us unless we allow our focus to shift away from the deep wells of loving Jesus and being loved by Him. Friend, let us be a people totally captivated by Him, caught up in His gaze and lost in His presence.

Faithfulness Leads to Breakthrough

Let's take a look at David's faithfulness. We discussed earlier how David was obedient even in the small things. He followed through for his father even in the simplest of requests, which gave him the opportunity to follow through for the Lord of Hosts in a big, notable way.

> Early in the morning David left the flock in the care of a shepherd, loaded up and set out, as Jesse had directed. He reached the camp as the army was going out to its battle positions, shouting the war cry. Israel and the Philistines were drawing up their lines facing each other. David left his things with the keeper of supplies, ran to the battle lines and asked his brothers how they were.
>
> 1 Samuel 17:20–22

We talked about this before, but I love it so much that I want to point it out a second time: I love that when David left home to bring food to his brothers he did not leave the sheep alone. He did not even leave them with his dad. He left them with another shepherd, someone who had the skill set to care for them properly. David was faithful to his commitment to shepherd that flock well, and this was pleasing to the Lord.

Upon arriving at the battlefield, David complied with the way things were done. He even left his supplies with the keeper of supplies. Though God had already anointed him as king over these men, he was faithful in following the rules and requirements on the battlefield. This, too, pleased the Lord.

David knew the battle taking place in the valley that day was about more than just fighting a natural battle. This was a battle over the mind and spirit, over the authority and identity of God's people. He was ready.

Isn't that what our battles are always over, my friend? When you stop and think about it you can see fear is out to distract you from who you are and blind you from the authority you walk in as Christ followers. Fear aims to get your eyes off Jesus and onto yourself. How can we follow through with the enormous God-call on our lives when the giant of fear is calling the shots? We cannot. And we will not. Because God's call is impossible to do in our own strength. It can only be accomplished when we rely on Him fully.

> I can do all things [which He has called me to do] through Him who strengthens and empowers me [to fulfill His purpose—I am self-sufficient in Christ's sufficiency; I am ready for anything and equal to anything through Him who infuses me with inner strength and confident peace].
>
> Philippians 4:13 AMP

And so here we see David stepping into this battle over the divine destiny and purpose of the people of God. They were like sheep without a shepherd being mocked and tormented by the giant of fear. Their eyes were not on their God, who was sending them, but on the giant of fear who was terrifying them. They had lost sight of the bigger picture.

But that is just what our flesh does, right? Our flesh sees things in the carnal. It sees what is in the natural realm, but our spirit sees with the lens of heaven, from an eternal vantage point. Our spirit sees the bigger picture, if you will. It sees God rightly, which remember, is what gives us the proper perspective on our own identity in Him.

Because he was led by his spirit and not by his flesh, David, though only a shepherd, stepped onto the battlefield, walked right up to Saul and told him, "Let no one lose heart on account of this Philistine; your servant will fight go and fight him" (1 Samuel 17:32). When Saul tried to shut David down, David told him a story about the time when a lion came and snatched up one of the sheep. He went after it and, with the Lord's help, rescued it. Then he told him about another time, when a bear came and snatched up the sheep. David fought it and killed it. He told Saul, "This will be no different." The point was clear: David had experience taking care of his flock when it was under attack. Whether sheep or people, David was faithful to his commitment and call to serve and protect. He could not stand by and watch as the enemy threatened those he cared for.

David's faithfulness—from the little things to the big—compelled him to take action. He knew what we are finding out: God does not give us eyes to see and ears to hear and then not equip us to do anything about what we see and hear, right? Our awareness demands a response and follow-through. That is precisely what David modeled for us in this chapter of the Bible. His obedience put action to his faith, and his faithfulness brought about the follow-through to the action.

As a result, David was not fearful; rather, he was fearless. He shook off the armor Saul had given him and took off running in faith onto the battlefield toward Goliath, declaring the goodness and nature of God almighty with every stride.

David said to the Philistine, "You come against me with sword and spear and javelin, but I come against you in the name of the LORD Almighty, the God of the armies of Israel, whom you have defied. This day the LORD will deliver you into my hands, and I'll strike you down and cut off your head. This very day I will give the carcasses of the Philistine army to the birds and the wild animals, and the whole world will know that there is a God in Israel. All those gathered here will know that it is not by sword or spear that the LORD saves; for the battle is the LORD's, and he will give all of you into our hands."

1 Samuel 17:45–47

David's follow-through led to the freedom of an entire army, who upon seeing this incredible moment "surged forward with a shout" (verse 52). They released their roar of breakthrough, tearing down the boundary line that once held them back and crossing over into their destiny full of faith. Their faith and their focus were restored as the grip of fear was removed. They surged forward in obedience and faithfulness with the veil of fear lifted because of this divine, supernatural act of David, a shepherd boy with a heart after God's heart.

This is the power of the Spirit of God inside us, friend. This is what His voice in us will accomplish. As we are faithful to the Lord, putting our hand to the plow of our own destiny and following through with the mandate on our lives, our flesh no longer responds to the grip of fear. Rather, our spirit will cry out with a roar of breakthrough, and the giant of fear will fall, slain, at our feet. Your faith puts a demand on the faithfulness of God.

Faithfulness Develops What Obedience Planted

In Part 2 of this book, we addressed what obedience establishes in us: a new perspective, a new posture and a new set

102

of priorities. In this one, we will take a close look at faithfulness and its significance in deepening our trust in the Lord, growing our character and giving us perseverance.

Faithfulness develops within us a trust in the Lord that runs deep. We become like that tree planted by the waters, sending out our roots toward the stream.

> But blessed is the one who *trusts in the LORD*, whose confidence is in Him. They will be like a tree planted by the water that sends out its roots by the stream. It does not fear when heat comes; its leaves are always green. It has no worries in a year of drought and never fails to bear fruit.
>
> Jeremiah 17:7–8, emphasis added

We may not always know why God allows us to go through hard times. We cannot see what He is doing. If we let it, fear will swoop in, in these seasons and wreak havoc in our thought life. We may find ourselves wondering, "Why would God let me go through this?" before our trust in the Lord begins to weaken.

When we are connected to the Lord and walk in faithfulness to Him, however, we will grow stronger and more confident every day. We will not fear when the enemy turns up the heat in our lives, because we cannot dry out as long as our root system taps into God. An outgrowth of our allegiance to the Lord, faithfulness develops in us a deep trust in Him, causing our roots to grow deep. Even in the desert and wilderness seasons of our lives, we will thrive, because we are nourished by springs of living water. We will continue to trust in Jehovah-Jireh, our Provider, because He is faithful. And through His faithfulness we can, in turn, be faithful ones.

"I Will Take the Hits for You"

My mother-in-law, Carole, is a picture of a modern-day faithful one. Her story is one of those that leaves your jaw on the ground for quite a while after you hear it. I remember when I first met my husband and he began to share with me about his mom. I was so inspired by her life that I could not wait to meet her. Now, after nearly two decades of being part of the family, I am still left speechless when I hear her retell the story, as I always learn new bits I had not heard before. In fact, when I launched my television program *Created for the Impossible*, I had her on as my very first guest for the pilot episode of the show.

Carole's story began with a newspaper article. She and her husband, Bob, sat in their beautiful suburban home in the metropolitan Detroit area one evening when Bob placed the front page of the newspaper on the table in front of Carole. The headline read "A House Stands Abandoned; Inside, a Woman Forgotten." It was an article about one of the many abandoned homes in the city of Detroit and the woman who was squatting in it.

The Lord moved on Carole's heart to go find this woman and share His love with her. That was all Carole needed to hear. In her bubbly, childlike manner, Carole said, "Okay, Jesus." Within two days, she had arranged to go with a friend into one of the most dangerous communities of Detroit, the Brightmoor district. Off she went from her beautiful suburban home to one of the most crime-ridden, precarious parts of Detroit to find a stranger the paper had referred to as "forgotten." And yet, she was absolutely unafraid.

Upon arrival, Carole knocked on and opened the front door—which was unlocked—of the abandoned home, but she did not see anyone inside. She returned to her car where her friend waited, and they decided to drive around to try to find her. Before long they spotted her, and Carole hopped out of the car to talk with her and let her know why they had come. They chatted for a little while, until out of nowhere the woman turned and ran away.

In that moment, Carole heard the Lord say, "Pursue! Pursue!" So, in obedience, Carole took off after the woman, walking purposely and waving her arms to get her attention, until she finally caught up to her. The woman had gone up on the front porch of a house, but when she saw Carole on the nearby street corner, she approached Carole, got right in her face and said, "If you don't leave me alone, I'm gonna get you." Carole stood firm. Full of perfect peace, Carole said repeatedly, "It's okay, Lovey. It's okay, Lovey." (Referring to her as "Lovey" was specifically what she felt very strongly from the Lord to say.)

All of a sudden, the woman hit Carole. Out of nowhere, she hit her in the chest, in the neck and in the shoulder. She hit her, and she pushed her.

Carole stood firm, full of the peace of God, not feeling even one of the blows. She stood firm, repeating those words, "It's okay, Lovey. It's okay, Lovey," until the woman gave up, turned and ran off again.

Feeling a release from the Lord, Carole returned to her car and sat down in the front passenger seat next to her friend. Trying to process what had just happened, she exhaled and said to the Lord, "Well, what was this all about, Jesus? What do You want me to learn from *this*?" She heard clear as day the Lord reply back to her, "If you stand on Me, I will take the hits for you."

It was from this moment that the Lord birthed a mission within Carole's heart. And in a subsequent vision He showed her a bright green light and the word *GO* in bold capital letters. That was all she needed to head off into the wild unknown to plant a mission in one of the most dangerous communities of Detroit.

One of my favorite parts of this story occurred within the first few weeks of Carole immersing herself in this community. Day after day, Carole walked the streets of Detroit talking to people, loving people and holding Bible studies in the cockroach-infested homes of some of the other "forgotten people" living in the community. Then one day Carole was approached by one of the community natives, who said to her, "I've seen people like you come in and out of here for years. I'll give you three months until you're gone." Carole just smiled her bright, sparkly smile and with that Jesus-twinkle in her eye said, "Okay." That was over two decades ago, and yet, Carole continues in that community, faithfully following through without fear on the mandate God placed on her life.

Her mission has operated in homes, storefronts, restaurants—wherever they would allow it. They have had big buildings and no building at all. But the common denominator was that the Lord told Carole to remain on one particular street, and so she did, whether she had a building or not. That is the street her mission operated on for over two decades. And do you know who helped her open it? The woman she saw in the paper that evening over coffee, the forgotten woman who hit and pushed her the day they first met. She ended up helping Carole open the mission and served there for years until she got cleaned up, got a job, moved back into a home and gave her life totally over to Jesus.*

*Laura Berman, "Berman: Column changes two lives," *Detroit News*, November 27, 2014, https://www.detroitnews.com/story/opinion/columnists/laura-berman/2014/11/27/berman-born-brightmoor/19568829/.

Our God is faithful. And He uses His faithful followers to be His hands and feet on the earth: "We are therefore Christ's ambassadors, as though God were making his appeal through us. We implore you on Christ's behalf: Be reconciled to God" (2 Corinthians 5:20).

Carole is a faithful one. She stepped out in obedience, which established in her a Jesus-perspective, a Jesus-posture of surrender and a Jesus set of priorities. And she has not looked back since. Her obedience empowered her faith, which led her to follow-through, establishing a lifestyle of faithfulness. Her one and only mission, she tells people, is to "love the Lord your God with all of your heart, all of your soul and all of your strength, and love your neighbor as yourself." While some might look back on the last two decades of her life and declare, "Mission accomplished," Carole presses on, faithfully running the race set before her. Her eyes are fixed on Jesus.

Carole's faithfulness to God was the stone that slayed, and continues to slay, the giant of fear that would stand in opposition of the mandate on her life to GO—capital G, capital O—into a dangerous community and love the people there like Jesus does. I am sure she would not even notice this Goliath on the horizon before her, and if she did, she would look him in the eye and tell him to go.

You see, the devil may try to set up giants along the battle line of our breakthrough, but when our focus is faithfulness to God we are fearless. If God is telling us to go forward and take the land of promise, then what should we fear? If God is for you, who can be against you? (See Romans 8:31.)

Often, we forget this truth in the moment. We take timid steps forward, see the giant, and retreat, as the army did. But God is raising up an army of fearless, faithful servants, an army of men and women full of His Spirit who are ready to surge forward in battle and take down their enemy. Will you be among them? If so, I can promise you this: Sure, you may experience some blows to your flesh from time to time. But as you stand on Him, He will take the hits for you.

DECLARE IT

No matter the cost, I will follow Christ. I will follow through on the GO of the gospel. I am a champion in Christ!

8

Faithful in the Unseen

The one who manages the little he has been given
with faithfulness and integrity will be promoted
and trusted with greater responsibilities.

Luke 16:10 TPT

Have you ever felt overlooked? Unseen? Like you have
this giant call of God bubbling up on the inside of
you, but no one else seems to be able to see it? You
are so excited about God's plan that it is all you can do to
keep it together, so to speak. But for now, all you can do is
wait on His timing.

You deeply desire God to reveal what His plan is for your
life and define what is simmering within you. As you wait
for the Holy Spirit to release what has been building inside
of you, you feel like a pressure cooker coming to full pressure. You are both excited and terrified all at the same time.

I know what the wilderness feels like. I know the frustra-
tion that can accompany carrying around the call of God. I

know what it is like to have to wait when you feel so ready to take steps forward, full of faith; to have your eyes fiercely focused on Jesus, praying with desperation and hope that He will motion you forward across the battle line of your life and that when He does, nothing will derail you—not even fear.

You see, part of why we fear the wilderness is that it triggers in us the fear of being overlooked. In this space we are more susceptible to the enemy's whispers that we are waiting because we are neither good enough nor qualified enough for what we long to spend our lives on. Ultimately, this is rooted in the fear of man, and it can easily consume us if we are not careful. We can get so caught up in man's opinion that we forget about our great big God, the one who created us for this particular time in His story.

My friend, as hard and lonely as this wilderness can feel, it is a very important place of growth. We often despise this place and the patience and the waiting it requires from us. But God wants you to be encouraged today that He has been planting seeds in you that are now beginning to develop, grow and bear fruit. Let me remind you again that even in seasons of waiting you are indeed being called over to the other side of your own battle line, the destiny line for your life. God is saying to you, "It is time. Fear not."

My friend, God hides us for a time and a season of development and refining, and now I believe Jesus is calling you out of the boat and onto the waters of the impossible with Him. Let's journey on.

Faithfulness Develops Character

The wilderness. The unseen. The hidden place. Whatever you call it, what you do in that space is so essential. It is critical, really, because this is the place of your development. This is the place where you begin to develop a habit of faithfulness, a pattern of behavior that allows you to declare with your life, "God, You are all that matters to me. My life is Yours." There, faithfulness begins to shape you and form your character.

The unseen, unknown wilderness seasons are the seasons of our reckoning. These are the seasons in which Jesus becomes our first love. He becomes our everything. And it is there where the Father molds us, forms us and shapes us. These seasons establish our foundation in Him as we continue to step out more into our calling, where the world can see us. Over time in the wilderness, we learn to appreciate and even crave set-apart time with God in which we rest in Him and He forms us more and more into the image of His Son.

After all, that is God's end goal: to mold us into the image of Christ. We are the clay, and He is our Potter. He is ever shaping us into sons and daughters who look like Jesus. This only happens through a process of maturity. For many of us, this makes us shake in our boots. Why? Because that word *process* sounds like it will take a long time. To be truthful, it will. The very definition of *process* speaks to a long journey ahead, one with multiple steps. But it is so necessary.

Though it may feel like it at times, this does not mean we will never transition from the unseen process and become activated into action. It just means God has the plan, and we do not. We simply need to fear not, yield our lives to the processes of God and allow Him to do as He pleases with our life.

David knew this. So much of David's development before and after Samuel anointed him as king over Israel occurred while he was alone in the fields tending the sheep. Resolute trust in God and His plan for David's life is the only thing that could have carried David from the moment of his anointing to the moment of his victory over Goliath years later and then to the even more distant moment at which he was crowned the king of Israel. Some scholars estimate that David waited for more than two decades for God to fulfill His promise to make him the king. He was able to wait faithfully, knowing that God was leading him through a process that would develop in him the particular and crucial set of character qualities that he would need in order to lead God's people well.

I am sure it was not easy. In his wilderness years David was overlooked even by his own dad. First Samuel 16 tells the story of Samuel's arrival to Jesse's home with the intention of anointing the next king of Israel. Jesse lined up all his sons, starting with the oldest, but never even considered his son David. He was left in the pastures with the sheep. Thankfully, God saw David when his father did not. As Samuel was looking at Jesse's oldest son, God told him: "Do not consider his appearance or his height, for I have rejected him. The LORD does not look at the things people look at. People look at the outward appearance, but the Lord looks at the heart" (1 Samuel 16:7).

The Scriptures tell us that years later David was still unseen by those who knew him most. When he stepped onto the battlefield in the Valley of Elah, David's older brother saw him and "burned with anger at him" (verse 28). He accused him of abandoning his flock (which was not true), of coming only to see the fight (also not true), and of being "conceited" and "wicked" in his heart. (Do I need to state the obvious here?) And David's response implies this was not the first

112

time he had to answer to his brother. I imagine him almost rolling his eyes as he replied, "Now what have I done?" (verse 29). After that, David turned and began a conversation with someone else. He had no time for entertaining the sort of people who would try to strike fear in his heart, instead of inspiring faithfulness to God.

The giant of fear tried to take his stand over and over in David's life. The enemy must have been quaking in his boots. But David knew this truth and lived it: The more we surrender ourselves to God, the more God fills us up with His presence, empowering and equipping us both for the battle and for the promised land beyond it.

Whether we are seen or unseen, if we are waiting or taking action, faithful faithfulness will lead us from victory to victory. We must always return to our one-on-one, intimate encounters with our Abba Father in His presence. In this "secret place" is where we are formed and our character is established (Psalm 91:1). We must value this place and prioritize it. It is where we learn to say, "Okay, Lord. You said there would be trouble but that I could live a life of cheer because you have overcome. I trust that my faithfulness will lead to joy, and that in joy Jesus gives us supernatural strength, making me resilient to life's twists and turns. I know that when I am abiding in You, fear doesn't stand a chance!"

Faithfulness Defeats the Fear of Man

For years I worked very hard to keep the peace. Plagued by the fear of man, I thought if I could just be likeable and remain in the good graces of everyone around me, I would avoid messes and conflict. Spoiler alert: It did not work. Staying quiet and sitting pretty is neither a recipe for relational health nor a shield against conflict. Before long, I was faced with a choice: crumble and cower before others or allow faithfulness to develop in me the boldness and courage I would need to defeat this giant once and for all. Since I am writing a book about overcoming fear, you can probably guess which I chose. That said, since I am writing a book about overcoming fear, I will be honest and tell you that choice was made reluctantly, at least at first.

I spent my twenties in the corporate world getting to know a variety of people, personally and as colleagues. I learned quickly that certain people did not like or get along with certain other people. There was strife and disagreement, and I wanted no part of it. I decided I would just fly under the radar and do all I could to keep the peace with all parties so I could live a life free of conflict. I told myself, "I can control my own actions, not the actions of anyone else. That means it is up to me to control the messes in my life, and avoiding conflict is the best way to do that." Hiding seemed like such a great plan at the time.

When I did have issues with people, I would simply come home and vent to my husband about it. To their face I was kind, happy and non-confrontational. You gotta keep the peace, right? Meanwhile, inside, my soul was being crushed a little more every day. Why? Because I was lying to myself and others, allowing fear to create a life of distortion and falsehood. It cost me dearly. Over time, I lost more and more of who I was and what I cared about. I was not standing on anything anymore. I became a shell of who I once was.

As I mentioned earlier, God used motherhood as the catalyst for this realization in my life. I was in my late twenties when I had my firstborn, and as I always like to tell her, she brought me back to life again. I looked into her eyes and realized keeping her safe and loving her well was more important to me than controlling everybody else's messes. It was more important even than trying to control my own. This began to shift my priorities and forced me to take off my "life is peachy" goggles and dare to stare reality in the eye. With her birth came the rebirth of all my dreams.

I took a look around and realized I had been hiding out. By trying to control messes and ease the storms of life by becoming a doormat at times, I was only painting the deck of the boat God was calling me to step out of. All around me was a life of false comfort, a life with no risk, a life consumed by the fear of man. But as motherhood began sinking in as my new normal—which was filled with risk and the unknown—I realized there is a whole world out there, and I am called to make a difference in it, if not for me, then for her, my baby girl.

Looking down at my daughter there in my arms, the fears I was consumed by began breaking down. I remember closing my eyes as I rocked her. The gliding sensation of my grandmother's rocking chair was like the rocking of a boat, and I listened with new ears for Jesus' voice over the waves. What I heard changed the trajectory of my life once and for all.

Jesus was calling me, and not from behind or even where I sat. He was out in the vast unknown before me calling me to take a step. "Come," I heard in my spirit. "Come follow Me." And all at once the dreams, the plans of God and the destiny on my life, it all came flooding to the forefront of my mind.

As I held my miracle girl in my arms, I had this overwhelming sensation that my Abba Father was doing the same, holding me and also beckoning me out of the life of faux safety and comfort. No more pleasing man and not fearing God.

It was time for me to embrace the reality before me: that God never asks us to keep the peace by remaining silent. He simply asks us to love, and sometimes love confronts. Sometimes love sets boundaries. But always, love has life. That is life out on the waters with Jesus, and I would stand with him outside of the boat I had built by vain effort.

All of those seeds God had planted in me when I was young began to break through the soil. In my teens I had been filled with passion and fire. I functioned with authority and identity. I was determined to shake history. In my twenties, I did everything I could just to keep from trembling in fear. But for the first time in a decade, I felt bold, courageous and ready to pursue the calling of God, whatever it required of me.

Unshakably Bold

Here is a little truth nugget for you: You can only shake history if you are willing to stand firm for what you believe and follow through on it. No one has shaken history without facing opposition and refusing to back down.

This requires us to be steadfast. I am not saying we should form an opinion and be obstinate or argumentative. We are still to remain teachable before God and those men and women in our lives who hold that sacred place of teaching us and holding us accountable. But there is so much deception taking place today that we must stay alert and ready to defend the truth when it is being compromised. As far as the world is concerned, we must know what we believe and why we believe it. We must be unafraid and unashamed of our stance, even when the fear of man walks up to the battle line and tries to throw us off course. Paul said, "For I am not ashamed of the gospel, because it is the power of God that brings salvation to everyone who believes" (Romans 1:16). We must have that kind of confidence in who and in whose we are.

Thankfully, faithfulness not only slays the giant of fear in our lives as we press forward in all that God has for us, but it also produces strength in us. It leads us into a bold and courageous lifestyle, the life God planned for us to live. Remember when He told Joshua, "Have I not commanded you? Be strong and courageous! Do not be terrified or dismayed (intimidated), for the Lord your God is with you wherever you go" (Joshua 1:9 AMP). Think about it. When we are faithful—filled with faith and forwardly moving in faith—we fear God, not man. Our faithfulness is unto the Lord and not unto man. As a result, we become His bold and courageous ambassadors, filled with trust and godly character.

Jesus modeled beautifully the divine empowerment available to all who believe in Him and put their trust in Him. His example is proof that we too can endure and can stand the test of time by remaining steadfastly faithful in what we believe. Because of His presence in our lives—in Spirit and in Word—we can be as He was: solid, unmovable, unshakable. We do not need to fear the storms or the winds of life or culture—whatever the enemy would try to throw at us. Just like that tree planted by streams of water, our roots grow deep like an anchor and allow us to draw in nourishment from His life flowing through our veins.

Make no mistake: We need that anchor. The giant of fear will bring all he has against us, and he will present himself as an unstoppable force. Just look at Goliath and the audacious armor he wore. Remember how Scripture described him:

> A champion named Goliath, who was from Gath, came out of the Philistine camp. His height was six cubits and a span.

He had a bronze helmet on his head and wore a coat of scale armor of bronze weighing five thousand shekels; on his legs he wore bronze greaves, and a bronze javelin was slung on his back. His spear shaft was like a weaver's rod, and its iron point weighed six hundred shekels. His shield bearer went ahead of him.

1 Samuel 17:4–7

Based on size alone, Goliath was nearly unstoppable, but armored for battle, he was unmatched. No one, not even David, could come close to his size or the quality of his armor.

This is what the enemy does in our lives. He draws our attention to others, and then he points out to us all their education, their looks and their qualifications. He points out to us all the things that they are and that we are not. He demoralizes us from the inside out through comparison and lies with just enough truth to seem real. And so often we bite. We give him an ear. We listen. We allow his words to run deep through our mind, and then into our heart. And we experience that shiver. You know, that cold shiver of fear, causing us to run in fear from our destiny. Before we know it, we are camped out on the sidelines of our own life, telling ourselves that if that other person is the standard, there is no way we could measure up to what God requires from us.

But it is all lies. All the enemy can do is lie to you, my friend. The way he compares your life to others and then uses it as "proof" to make you feel inadequate? It is a cheap shot. And it is time his lies be dismantled.

We can start by looking again at David. He was a shepherd boy who showed up to a battlefield still carrying his staff and wearing his shepherd's pouch. He did not even change his clothes to try to fit in on the field. He was who he was, and he was not intimidated by anyone. His mind did not even go there. Why? Well, because his mind was not consumed with the fear of man, to put it bluntly. His mind was not polluted with the fear of being less-than. He functioned with clarity on his position and his identity. He was not insecure. He was who he was, and that was enough for him, because he knew it was enough for God. David was unshakable because he was anchored in and nourished by his walk with God, and he understood his calling. Do we not all hope for the same clarity on our identity and what God is forming us to be?

That hope is your reality. Remember, David is a representation of the spirit—of your renewed spirit through Christ. Your spirit is not intimidated by man. Your spirit fears God. Your spirit is confident in the Lord, in the God who is sending you. It is not focused on or scared of the giant before you. Your spirit resonates with God's Spirit within and remains determined to follow through, because it knows you have been anointed by God for such a time as this. As a result, when you are led by the Spirit, you will fear not. You will be able to show up just as you are, flaws and all. You will be able to put your hand to the plow of your life and do it scared. You will press on toward the goal on the path marked out for you, and you will allow God to be enough. He qualifies you. He calls you. He is forming you and shaping you and empowering you, whether you see it or not, and whether others see it or not. Remember, your faith puts a demand on God's faithfulness.

God has never withdrawn His love or His plan for you. He is simply ready for you to say yes to His call, step forward in obedience and faithfully show up day-in and day-out so He can partner with you to change the world.

DECLARE IT

I will focus more on my God, who is sending me, than the giant of fear in front of me. I fear God, not man. I am a champion in Christ!

9

Faithful in the Fire

Blessed is the one who perseveres under trial because, having stood the test, that person will receive the crown of life that the Lord has promised to those who love him.

James 1:12

Is it enough for you to continue living in the shadow of the giant of fear, even though God has better things for you on the other side? Is it enough to trust Him with your life, until He calls you to act on your trust that He will save it from harm? Is it enough for you to obey in all things, except when He prompts you to go to battle?

I cannot answer these questions for you. No one can. But I can promise you that they are questions everyone must face. David faced them. Other giants of faith in the Scriptures have faced them. Other men and women today—I am raising my hand—have had to answer them. And I will tell you this: How you answer will change the course of your whole life.

David would still likely have been a man after God's heart without Goliath, but he would not have been a giant-killer, and he would not have ruled over God's people in the promised land. Because he gave his obedience legs through action and followed through faithfully, Goliath fell. David learned, once again, that God would honor his faithfulness by being faithful in return. And his people were able to live in the land God had prepared for them.

You see, the only way to overcome fear and experience a victorious life is to engage it and persevere until you find yourself victorious. You cannot win as long as you cower. Eventually, fear will just get louder. Over time, it will take more ground. One way or another, you are going to have to decide either to face fear or to accept a life hiding in the shadows. If you want the former, if you want to live in the abundant life God has waiting for you, you are going to have to step out in faith, weapons in hand.

You will not have to do it alone. If God is for you, who can stand against you (Romans 8:31)? If God has a life of freedom and victory waiting for you on the other side of the battle line, not even death can stop Him.

Faithfulness Defeats the Fear of Death

"For such a time as this." We love to say this in our Christian circles, but it is easy to forget that for Esther it was not just a reminder of God's providential timing and positioning. It was a powerful call to action, deep calling out to deep to ensure and solidify the preservation of the people of God for all time. Esther's story is no less than a demonstration of the weapon of quiet faithfulness being wielded to slay the giant of the fear of death. She was faithful to her people and to her Lord, even in the face of grave danger, and it saved not only her life but an entire nation.

You see, Esther, a Jew, found herself in a position she never imagined. An orphan girl, Esther was raised by her cousin, Mordecai. As an adult she found herself unexpectedly queen of Egypt. Mordecai had instructed her to keep her family background and nationality a secret from everyone in the palace, which she did faithfully (see Esther 2:20). Then something happened that forced her to reveal her full identity.

In Esther 3 we read that Haman, one of the king's men, had just been promoted. The king elevated him, "giving him a seat of honor higher than that of all the other nobles" (verse 1). All the royal officials at the king's gate bowed to him. Mordecai also stood at the gate, but he would not bow. This made Haman furious.

> Then the royal officials at the king's gate asked Mordecai, "Why do you disobey the king's command?" Day after day they spoke to him but he refused to comply. Therefore they told Haman about it to see whether Mordecai's behavior would be tolerated, for he had told them he was a Jew.
>
> Esther 3:3–4

It was not enough for Haman to kill only Mordecai. No, he wanted to wipe out Mordecai's entire people. If that one man would not bow because of the God he served, it stood to reason they could encounter this again. Haman's pride was too great to tolerate such a thing.

> Then Haman said to King Xerxes, "There is a certain people dispersed among the peoples in all the provinces of your

kingdom who keep themselves separate. Their customs are different from those of all other people, and they do not obey the king's laws; it is not in the king's best interest to tolerate them. If it pleases the king, let a decree be issued to destroy them, and I will give ten thousand talents of silver to the king's administrators for the royal treasury."

Esther 3:8–9

The king was in favor of this request. He gave Haman his signet ring and said, "Keep the money . . . and do with the people as you please" (verse 11). So Haman drafted an edict for every province and in every language with the order to "destroy, kill and annihilate all the Jews—young and old, women and children" (verse 13).

When Mordecai heard of this order he was in great distress. He tore his clothes and walked through the city wailing (Esther 4:1). In all the provinces, the Jewish people were in mourning. They wept and fasted, crying out to God for help. Eventually Esther received word from her cousin about this edict, and she was alarmed.

It seemed Esther had only two options available, and both led to death. If she remained quiet, without standing up to Haman, she and her countrymen would die by the edict. If she approached her husband without an official summons, the king had the legal power to put her to death for her act of insubordination. To make matters bleaker, the king had not called for her in a full month. She had no guarantee he would welcome her presence instead of condemn her for it.

Mordecai reminded Esther that her only hope—the only real option for her and the people she represented—was to gamble with her own life by approaching her husband, the king. Her only chance was to pray that he would decide to extend his golden scepter to her, sparing her life, so that she could present her case. It was a slim chance, yes, but what if it was exactly what God had in mind?

> When Esther's words were reported to Mordecai, he sent back this answer: "Do not think that because you are in the king's house you alone of all the Jews will escape. For if you remain silent at this time, relief and deliverance for the Jews will arise from another place, but you and your father's family will perish. And who knows but that you have come to your royal position for such a time as this?"
>
> Esther 4:12–14

I love that Mordecai acknowledged that regardless of what Esther did, God's people would be saved. His suggestion, however, that she might be divinely positioned to be an instrument of deliverance for God's beloved people clearly got the wheels turning in her mind. She mulled it over and responded with wisdom and with a plan that would require her faithfulness, as well as the people's.

> Then Esther sent this reply to Mordecai: "Go, gather together all the Jews who are in Susa, and fast for me. Do not eat or drink for three days, night or day. I and my attendants will fast as you do. When this is done, I will go to the king, even though it is against the law. And if I perish, I perish."
>
> Esther 4:15–16

Esther realized that she was indeed positioned by God "for such a time as this." She was not in the palace by chance but rather divine destiny. Like David, she had stumbled upon a battle—a battle over the lives of God's people. The light-bulb of faith went on, and she called her people to action, to faithfulness. She called upon them to follow through on their commitment to God by fasting so she could enter the king's chambers, facing death, knowing that she had done her part and the rest was up to God. Whatever happened after that, she would have been faithful. She would have put her hand to the plow of her faith and showed up.

Esther followed through, even to the point of impending death: "If I perish, I perish." Her faithfulness to the Lord and to her people was the weapon she wielded against the giant fear in this story, the fear of death. Unsurprisingly, it struck a death blow.

After three days she slipped on the royal robe her husband had given her and stood in the doorway of the king. She stood tall, awaiting the king's acknowledgment. Would she be put to death? Or would she be extended mercy?

> The king was sitting on his royal throne in the hall, facing the entrance. When he saw Queen Esther standing in the court, he was pleased with her and held out to her the gold scepter that was in his hand. So Esther approached and touched the tip of the scepter.
>
> Esther 5:1–2

Yes, Esther was indeed spared, along with the entire nation of Israel. Because she humbly honored her cousin's counsel, considered the plight of her people and acted in faithfulness to God, the Lord was able to use her to save His people and demonstrate His love. With one fell swoop, Esther cut down the fear of death for good.

In your hand, faithfulness holds the same power against the giant of fear looming over you. So slip on your royal robe, my friend, your robe of righteousness. Remember the royal position you hold as the bride of Christ, the righteousness of God in Christ (2 Corinthians 5:21), and dare to look that giant of fear in the eye today. Even he cannot deny your royal position. It is written:

> I delight greatly in the LORD; my soul rejoices in my God. For he has clothed me with garments of salvation and arrayed me in a robe of his righteousness, as a bridegroom adorns his head like a priest, and as a bride adorns herself with her jewels.
>
> Isaiah 61:10

There Is Freedom in the Fire

"There is freedom in the fire," my dear friend Mary declared as she stood before a room of women at a recent conference we ministered at together. She had just told the story of Shadrach, Meshach and Abednego, three men who were bound and thrown in a fiery furnace because of their faithfulness to God:

> Furious with rage . . . Nebuchadnezzar said to them, "Is it true, Shadrach, Meshach and Abednego, that you do not serve my gods or worship the image of gold I have set up? Now when you hear the sound of the horn, flute, zither, lyre, harp, pipe and all kinds of music, if you are ready to fall down and worship the image I made, very good. But if you do not worship it, you will be thrown immediately into a blazing furnace. Then what god will be able to rescue you from my hand?"
>
> Shadrach, Meshach and Abednego replied to him, "King Nebuchadnezzar, we do not need to defend ourselves before you in this matter. If we are thrown into the blazing furnace,

the God we serve is able to deliver us from it, and he will deliver us from Your Majesty's hand. But even if he does not, we want you to know, Your Majesty, that we will not serve your gods or worship the image of gold you have set up."

Daniel 3:13–18

Shadrach, Meshach and Abednego were unwilling to bow to the human king who demanded their worship. They were unwilling to compromise their beliefs in the face of opposition. They were faithful to God, even unto death. Talk about follow-through.

Hebrews 11:6 says, "Without faith it is impossible to please God, because anyone who comes to him must believe that he exists and that he rewards those who earnestly seek him." That Scripture was written hundreds of years after Shadrach, Meshach and Abednego lived, but these men testified to its truth. They were unafraid to stand firm on who they were as God's people. They were faithful in the fire of opposition and in the face of death. What could have, and probably should have, gripped them with fear—fear of man, fear of being misunderstood, conflict, death, etc.—only seemed to solidify their position. They were faithful to the very end in their service and allegiance to the Lord. They were willing to follow through, even if it meant death, because they trusted that God was on their side, regardless of the outcome.

So often we fear opposition, and we fear being misunderstood. We loathe confrontation. But I love what the guys said to King Nebuchadnezzar: "We do not need to defend ourselves before you in this matter" (verse 16). In other words, "We understand that we will never see eye-to-eye in this. But we know God is on our side. Even if He doesn't intervene and save our lives, God will defend Himself." They had been obedient, and they showed faithfulness in refusing to compromise their beliefs. They knew their action, and explanation of allegiance to God, said all they needed to say. God Himself would say the rest. What a beautifully firm stance to take.

As a result, they had an encounter with the presence of God in the fire. Whether it was Jesus with them, or an angel of God, they were not alone. In a place of fierce opposition, pain, torment and death, they were alive, unbound and walking with the presence of God. And they came out unharmed! Their faithfulness yielded fearlessness.

Whatever furnace you are facing—or maybe it is the giant of fear waving a burning torch in front of you—there is freedom in the fire, because God is with you in the fire. Even in the midst of opposition, even when you think the battle might kill you, you are not alone. The very personification of victory is by your side. "And be sure of this: I am with you always, even to the end of the age" (Matthew 28:20 NLT).

You need to know that God has not promised you a life absent of trials, but He has promised you a hope and a future. God wants you to fear not the trial before you. Instead, He wants you to stand firm on Jesus and what He did for you. He desires your character be so rooted in Him that you are firm in what you believe and why you believe it.

Many refer to this as part of one's worldview, and that is not wrong, but I say this is your God-view. It is your stance on who God is in your life, on who Jesus is and what He did for you. Know that—really, really know that—and you will not be shaken by the fiercest threat or opposition. Know that, and the giant of fear will lose all his power over you.

If you have not stepped out of the boat and responded in obedience to His call on your life, today is the day. Today is the day that roar of breakthrough begins to rise up from within you. Can you feel it there? Do you sense your strength in the Lord growing more and more? I pray you do. Better yet, I decree over you right now as you are reading that supernatural strength is rising up inside of you. He who is in you is greater than he who is in the world, and He will honor His promise to guard your heart and reward your faithfulness. You no longer need to be concerned about who sees you. Instead, you can focus on who sends you. You do not need recognition because you have received reconciliation. God is for you, so who can be against you?

Friend, you are a faithful one. Yes, I declare it over you now. I prophesy to your very soul right now: You are a faithful one! It is time you hit the reset button on your life and allow the new mercies of your heavenly Father to wash over you now. It is time for you to walk out a renewed lifestyle of faithfulness that will produce fearlessness. Starting today, right here and now, you are faithful in the fire and faithful in the storm, knowing that since you are God's beloved, His arms are around you, keeping you from harm. Starting today, you are fearless!

DECLARE IT

I will dare slip on my royal robe and look fear in the eye, standing tall in Christ yet humbly laying my life down for His name's sake. I am fearless in my faithfulness. I am a champion in Christ!

PART 4

Weapon #3
STEWARDSHIP

10

Why Stewardship?

The earth is the LORD's, and everything in it, the
world, and all who live in it; for he founded it on
the seas and established it on the waters.

Psalm 24:1–2

Have you ever had one of those dreams where everything seems to be going wrong? You are supposed
to be somewhere by a certain time—work, a class,
the airport—but for some reason everything is working
against you, preventing you from getting where you need to
be on time? Your alarm does not go off, your car will not
start or you get distracted by a myriad of bizarre encounters along the way. You know, like your old boss showing
up at your house to make pancakes, and you get caught up
in conversation. Or, instead of driving to work you decide
to walk, and when you are halfway there you look at your
watch and realize you will never make it on time. You start

to run and realize you are barefoot, and your feet hurt so badly that all you want to do is call in sick for the day. But, of course, your cell phone is a banana.

I had one of these dreams just the other night. Mine involved the town I lived and worked in nearly a decade ago, my old workplace, a motorcycle, high heels, getting lost on the way to the airport, and a broken cellphone that could not make calls but displayed the countdown to when my plane was set to take off. If I remember correctly, my phone was smiling at me, too, as it counted off the minutes until I missed my flight. I woke up with a very real sense of panic that I was not going to make it onto the plane in my dream.

This type of panic is rooted in our fear of failure and missing the mark. It is a "so close and yet so far" kind of fear. But there is good news. When we are good stewards, we can avoid this kind of fear altogether. Why? Because stewardship means we are managing what we have been given as best we can; we do not own it or the responsibility for it. This gets us off the hook and frees us up to live our life in pursuit of God without carrying the weight of His plan on our shoulders.

When we function as a steward, we acknowledge our partnership with heaven. We are not alone in this. We are being cheered on by the great cloud of witnesses, those who have run their race and passed on to glory, all celebrating our successes and championing us even in our missteps. They know, as we do, that Christ has already laid out our path. All we have to do is follow it—follow Him—until the end. This removes the pressure.

> Therefore, since we are surrounded by such a great cloud of witnesses, let us throw off everything that hinders and the sin that so easily entangles. And let us run with perseverance the

race [Christ] *marked out for us*, fixing our eyes on Jesus, the pioneer and perfector [*"author and finisher,"* AMP] of faith.

Hebrews 12:1–2, emphasis added

As stewards, it is not our job to take responsibility for God's plan working out. Instead, stewardship means we are here on the earth doing all we can do to focus on what we have been given by God to manage. At the end of the day we can take a deep breath knowing we are doing the best we can—and that is all God is asking of us. This knowledge stops fear dead in its tracks.

Good Stewardship Is Powerful

Here is a little nugget of truth for you: The devil is terrified of becoming obsolete. He is so scared of failing to stop you, of not having a voice in your life and in your destiny. Is it not interesting that we experience the same fear of failure, irrelevance and of not being heard? It is no coincidence. That fear we feel—the fear that often manifests in crazy running-out-of-time dreams—is a mere projection of the enemy's fear of becoming obsolete and losing his power over your life. That is right; the enemy is projecting his fears onto you. Why? Because he has already been defeated by the power of the cross. If you let him, he will spend your lifetime diligently attacking your faith with fear so you never fully embrace that truth.

Stewardship is a weapon because it means we realize God owns everything, and we are resolved to manage what we have been given. Robert Morris gave a wonderful sermon in January 2019 on stewardship. In it he taught, "Stewardship is the management of the property of another." When it comes to our role on this planet, he said, we need to remember "we are not the owner . . . we are the steward."* James 1:17 tells us, "Every good and perfect gift is from above, coming down from the Father of the heavenly lights, who does not change like shifting shadows."

Everything we have is not ours; it comes to us on loan from our heavenly Father, and we are here to be His stewards by managing His property, His time, His resources and even the gifts, talents and skills He has given us. With that understanding, the question, as Morris points out, is not "Are we owners or stewards?" but "Are we *good* stewards?"

If stewardship is a divine partnership with God, then good stewardship means we are functioning on God's system and not the world's system. Good stewardship produces specific fruit in our lives. Much like obedience and faithfulness, stewardship keeps us focused, disciplined and intentional in our pursuit of God's plan. It unlocks supernatural provision from the Lord, not just of material resources but of health, favor, hope and blessing. When we are walking in these supernatural gifts, what could we fear? How could fear make us afraid, when we have all that we need from on High?

Stewardship Slays the Giant

There is a common pattern to the enemy's attempt to shake our confidence and derail our obedience and faithfulness. I have experienced it and witnessed it many times. It often happens this way: God has given you a big vision, and you are ready to run ahead, trusting the Lord with your destiny. You

*Gatewaychurchtv, "Robert Morris–Good Stewards–Beyond Blessed," You-Tube video, 35:23, January 28, 2019, https://www.youtube.com/watch?v=UFsx7EB7ODE&feature=youtu.be.

recognize the bigness of it all, and you have acknowledged that you cannot do it on your own. You tell God that for it to come to pass, He will pave the way and do the impossible. And you really trust that He will come through, because He is faithful.

Then out of nowhere something small catches you off guard. Maybe it is a text from a friend or family member that undercuts your courage. Perhaps it is a little comment from your spouse, who snaps at you after a long day at work. He apologizes later, but the damage is done. Suddenly you do not feel so bold anymore. You begin to worry that you had it wrong somehow. Your mind swirls with a thousand questions, like, *What if this battle is not the Lord's but rather a fight I picked with the enemy because of my own insecurities? What if this is selfish? What if I got the timing wrong, and God is not actually behind me?* Before you know it, your courage has been undermined with fear—a threat you did not even see coming. You begin to sink inside, and you want to cower and pull back. What you do next to steward God's call in the shadow of the giant of fear will change everything.

Even David experienced this scenario. In the process to getting to Goliath, the enemy sent other fear-giants to catch him off guard and steal his courage and resolve. I would suggest the enemy knew David was not afraid of Goliath. David feared God, and this giant was clearly in defiance of Him. David understood the problem at hand was bigger than him, and he knew that God Almighty would come through. For David, it was not a matter of *if* God would give him the victory over Goliath but *how*. He walked in a supernatural sense of security because he understood God had called him to steward the gifts and experience he had been given in order to defeat the giant. As he approached the battle line, I imagine he was asking the Lord:

How are You going to come through today, God?

Who will remove this disgrace from Israel?

Recognizing David's obedience and faithful action, the enemy realized his only chance to shake God's servant was to make him take on the burden of battle alone. He fell back on his tried-and-true strategy of using other people and relationships to try to undermine David's resolve and cause him to question whether or not God was really on his side, whether or not God would ultimately own the responsibility for the victory that day.

For his first attack, the enemy used David's brother. As you walk with the Lord and live out the plan He has for you, you will discover—if you have not already—that the enemy loves to leverage your relationships with people you know, and oftentimes, people you trust to cause you to become fearful. It is no surprise that the enemy's first giant to step into David's path was someone close to David.

If you remember, David approached the battlefield with two parallel mandates. We see the mandate from David's earthly father, which was the reason David was there. But as the story unfolds, we can also see the mandate from David's heavenly Father. It is important to keep in mind that he did not go to the battlefield on assignment from the Lord; he went to the battlefield on assignment from his earthly father. Through David's brother, the enemy used this to try to make David think that his conflict was not God-ordained but self-appointed and prideful. Remember this exchange:

David asked the men standing near him, "What will be done for the man who kills this Philistine and removes this disgrace from Israel? Who is this uncircumcised Philistine that he should defy the armies of the living God?"

They repeated to him what they had been saying and told him, "This is what will be done for the man who kills him."

When Eliab, David's oldest brother, heard him speaking with the men, he burned with anger at him and asked, "Why have you come down here? And with whom did you leave those few sheep in the wilderness? I know how conceited you are and how wicked your heart is; you came down only to watch the battle."

1 Samuel 17:26–28

David's own brother was tearing him down in the same way Goliath had torn down the army. It was the same giant of fear presenting in a unique way to hit him where it hurts, so to speak, and call into question David's faith in God's faithfulness.

As we discussed in an earlier chapter, David was not thrown off by his brother. Where so many of us would have succumbed to the flesh and allowed our hurt feelings to set us back, David's response was instant: "Not this again. What are you talking about?" (verse 29). He did not try to defend his motives. He did not address the personal attack. He knew the mandate that brought him to the battlefield, and he had already perceived God's mandate for him, given Goliath's defiance and heresy. David simply turned his back on this giant of fear presenting through his brother. He moved along and went back stewarding God's character and His sheep.

The enemy was not about to give up that easily. The next giant of fear came clothed in the robes of leadership. *Perhaps*, the enemy must have thought, *King Saul would be able to convince David to give up his fight against Goliath. Perhaps his king would succeed at making David question whether or not God had his back.* Saul sent for David, and this is their exchange:

> David said to Saul, "Let no one lose heart on account of this Philistine; your servant will go and fight him."
>
> Saul replied, "You are not able to go out against this Philistine and fight him; you are only a young man, and he has been a warrior from his youth."

> verses 32–33

Just like Goliath and David's brother, Saul called into question David's ability, identity and calling. He targeted the very things David was stewarding: his gifts, his talents and his God-given purpose and anointing. Why? So David would back down in fear.

As we have seen throughout this book, David is a beautiful representation of our spirit. He did not give in to fear. Fear did not have a voice in his life because his focus was on the Lord. His response is powerful:

> But David said to Saul, "Your servant has been keeping his father's sheep. When a lion or a bear came and carried off a sheep from the flock, I went after it, struck it and rescued the sheep from its mouth. When it turned on me, I seized it by its hair, struck it and killed it. Your servant has killed both the lion and the bear; this uncircumcised Philistine will be like one of them, because he has defied the armies of the living God. The LORD who rescued me from the paw of the

lion and the paw of the bear will rescue me from the hand of this Philistine."

Saul said to David, "Go, and the LORD be with you."

verses 34–37

David knew how to steward this mandate from the Lord because he was an experienced shepherd who knew that everything he had came from, and belonged to, God. He had stewarded sheep and protected them from harm. He had stewarded his anointing from God through Samuel, even while waiting to be crowned king. He was a good shepherd, a good steward, and he knew how to function under God's ownership and direction because he had been doing it for years.

It is no surprise that David refused the armor Saul offered him. Instead, he carried his shepherd's rod onto the battlefield, along with his shepherd's pouch and sling (verse 40). He used what he had at hand, what he had already been given by God Himself. They were not only weapons but symbols—for David, for the soldiers, and for all of us throughout history who read his story—of David's stewardship over the mandate and calling of God on his life. Even the enemy's best attempt to undercut David's courage could not compete with that.

What Does Your Giant Look Like?

What is God calling you to steward? Have you identified it yet? If so, it is likely you have personal experience with the enemy's tactic of using close relationships to derail your pursuit of God's mandate on your life.

This occurred for me as I was pursuing the plans of God on my life to launch a television show. I was not even so much afraid of the enormity of the show itself. It was clearly bigger than me, so I knew my God would have to steer the ship. But then out of nowhere I was buffeted by consistent, small, out-of-nowhere jabs from people around me. Even though in most cases they were unintentional, each jab hit right where it hurt, attacking my ability, my identity and my calling.

It was incredibly painful and disheartening, but it did not stop me. Because I was walking in obedience and faithfulness and knew beyond a shadow of a doubt that I was stewarding the call of God on my life, the giant of fear did not get me off course. His shouts were no more than whispers. His intimidation was not nearly as intimidating as the assignment itself. He could not redirect my steps because my eyes were fixed on the one calling me, not the giant attempting to derail me.

As of today we have produced over fifty episodes and are beginning our third season of filming. We moved from the studio environment, where the episodes were produced by a network, to filming 100 percent out of studio, and I now hold the position of host and executive producer. Let me remind you: This is not something I saw coming. I did not spend my life waiting for the day I could host and produce a television program. In fact, I would rather have avoided it because it is so public, and I, an introvert, would prefer to sit behind a laptop and write books about being created for the impossible and slaying giants of fear. But that was not God's plan.

God's plan was, and is, for me to live the messages I preach. I need to experience all the knee-shaking "I don't understand why God would choose me for this" experiences firsthand so that I can adequately convey God's heart for people, for you.

His heart is this: God is not looking for fancy. He is not looking for the ones who have it all together. He simply scans the earth looking to and fro for the ones who love His Son, who have laid their lives down to follow Christ. He looks for lovers, for those who are not so full of themselves that they lack any glimmer of Jesus flowing out of them. He is looking for you, the faithful one. He is looking for the stay-at-home mom. The working dad. The career-minded woman. The unlikely son who maybe messed up a lot in the past, but you are eager today.

Friend, His eyes are on you, so here is what you can do: Dream a little today. Ask the Lord to give you a new vision, restoring to you fresh passion and fire for His Word and for His plans for your life. Decide today that God's plan is enough and that what He has given you to steward, you will hold before Him as an offering of worship. He is the owner; you are the manager, and your aim is to focus fiercely on Jesus, the author and perfector, the one who inspires the impossible within you. He is the one who broke the curse and opened up the pathway to eternity for you, the pathway to the Father's heart and will for your life—yes, your little, amazing life, supernaturally infused with the fire of God's enormous plan, which is now becoming your new normal.

DECLARE IT

I resolve today to press onward in the call of God on my life, ignoring the subtle jabs and deliberate assaults of the enemy and fiercely focused on Jesus before me. I am a champion in Christ!

11

What Is in Your Hand?

His master replied, "Well done, good and faithful
servant! You have been faithful with a few things;
I will put you in charge of many things. Come
and share your master's happiness!"

Matthew 25:21

The ultimate goal of every Christ-follower is to hear
these words from the Father at the end of our life:
"Well done, good and faithful servant." It is a wonderful goal, and one we should work toward daily. But we
do not have to wait until eternity to reach it. It is possible to
hear these words while we are here on the earth as we steward well and care for the resources God has given us today.

The first step to good stewardship is, well, taking the first
step. Often we set aside or bury what we have for fear that
it is not enough. We compare ourselves and our resources
today with what we hope to be given in the future, and we

tell ourselves, "My gift is not big enough. If I step out now I will fail." But we need to remember that what we have now is what we were given by God to steward. He has given us all He wants us to have in this moment. Multiplication—the "more" from God—comes as we invest what He has delivered into our hands. As we show ourselves faithful to steward that, then God will give us more.

In Matthew 25 we read a story Jesus told to help people understand what good stewardship, what Kingdom stewardship, looks like. In the parable, a man was preparing to go on a journey, so he called three of his trusted servants to his office and gave them some of his money to invest for him. The master gave each of the three men different quantities based on their ability and experience and instructed them to use the money wisely.

Two of the servants invested their money and saw growth. When the master came back, they proudly returned to him his initial investment plus the increase. To these men, the master proclaimed, "Well done, good and faithful servant! You have been faithful with a few things; I will put you in charge of many things. Come and share your master's happiness!" (verses 21, 23).

The servant who had been given the smallest quantity buried his instead of investing it. He had operated in fear and never invested the money he was given in order to yield an increase. He was so proud to return with the original sum, none lost or used, that it did not occur to him that he should have stewarded the master's resources differently. He wrongly assumed it was better to return with something rather than nothing. Instead of sowing—which leads to harvest—he hid it away. Instead of stewarding what he had been given, he sat idle. As a result, instead of "well done," this servant received a rebuke, and what he had been given was taken from him and given to another.

The Parable of the Talents seems to address financial stewardship, but it is also about sowing and reaping, which has to do with more than just money. Being a good steward means sowing whatever God has given you and then reaping the harvest of it. Your gifting, your skill set, the assignment God has called you to, your time and even the anointing on your life are all gifts from your heavenly Master to be stewarded during your time here on earth. God has entrusted you with these resources—with His resources—because He believes you are faithful. When you put them to use, rather than hide them, only then will you see an increase and harvest.

God does not want you to live in fear and not use what you have. He wants you to invest it, to give it away, to pour it out. His design is that your life would overflow with Him so that the lost may be filled with the knowledge of God. As you are obedient to do your part, God will melt away your fears and also bring the increase in your life. This is the Kingdom way.

You Have to Let Go

Financial stewardship is no more important than stewarding the other resources God has given us, but it can be helpful in understanding these principles because it provides a tangible, quantifiable example of what it looks like to sow what God has given us and believe He will bring the increase. For me, trusting God when my husband and I were struggling with our budget was a terrifying but powerful trust fall scenario that taught me an incredible lesson about sowing and reaping. Right when I thought I was falling backward into nothingness, God reached out and caught me, and it has changed my life.

Not so long ago I went to the bank to set up a new account. This in itself was a big deal, because it represented a major leap of faith forward into investing in God's plan for my life instead of clinging to my finances. For years, I had been obedient to God's call. Anything He asked of me, I said, "Okay, Lord." I had been faithful. I was showing up day-in and day-out, putting my hand to the plow of God's destiny on my life. I had even learned to ignore and overcome that giant of fear trying to derail me. But there was still one little area that I had not surrendered to God—my finances—and I had gotten to the point in my journey where God wanted all of me. Stepping through the doors to the bank to set up that account was a huge step forward in learning to steward, instead of bury, an important resource God had given to me.

While I was there, the banker asked me about my five-year plan, and I just sort of laughed. You know how people talk about surviving near-death experiences and seeing their life flash before their eyes? I was not in any kind of danger in that moment, but the question triggered a flashback to the last few years of my life.

After my husband, Donovan, and I decided when my son was born that I would not return to the workforce, our income was cut in half. Really, it was cut by more than half, as I was earning a higher salary than Donovan at the time. For eight years we lived tightly. Month to month, we trusted the Lord just to cover our bills each month, and He was faithful. But our goal was to at some point be able to earn enough to cover our bills, break even, flourish and save.

We were thankful for God's miraculous provision for eight years, but we knew some of the responsibility for our future financial stability was on our shoulders. Donovan began to look for other jobs that might increase our household income, and in the process, he discovered he was suited for an industry he had never before considered: home inspections. At just the right time, the door opened for him to launch his own business and step into a career that he was truly made for. In the beginning, he worked a full-time schedule at his corporate job and took appointments for his home inspection business on his days off. Within only a few months, however, he was earning more than enough to cover our monthly deficit. We were so thankful. For the first time in eight years we were breaking even each month!

Almost immediately, the Lord began to bring to mind an image of my hands, fingers clinched tightly as though holding on to something. In my spirit I would hear the Lord say, "Let go." I knew right away what it meant, but it took a little time for me to admit it: God was asking me to invest financially in the ministry He had called me to. He was asking me to let go of my need to control our finances so closely in order to begin stepping out in greater faith, not just to do what I was called to do but to bring others in to help increase the work it could accomplish.

Just thinking about that season causes tears to well up in my eyes. I always loved listening to people tell stories about how the Lord blessed them financially, how when they gave something away God blessed them in return. As much as I loved these tales of God's faithfulness, I never imagined I could have one of them. Deep down, I wrote it off as a blessing I would never get to enjoy. "That happened for them, but I fear it will not happen for me," I told myself.

When the Holy Spirit began to prompt me to let go of my need to control our finances—and to let go of some of our financial margin by investing it in the Kingdom—I was terrified. To be honest, I did not even fully understand why it mattered. Radical obedience had become normal in all other areas of my life. Why did God need me to be obedient in this?

Through a lot of tears and a lot of time on my face crying out to God, I realized something important: The only reason I was hesitant to be obedient to God in the area of our finances was because I had focused my attention not on Jehovah-Jireh, the Lord who Provides, but on the giant of fear. He was standing on my destiny line, and he was screaming his lies and insults so loudly that I could scarcely hear the voice of God inviting me to cross over.

"Let go, Krissy."

"You can do it, Krissy."

"You can trust Me to have your back."

"I believe in you."

"I am with you always."

Once I knew what I was really fighting, I could begin to develop a resistance to his attacks. I stepped out in obedience to God's mandate to steward what He had given me; I was faithful to follow through with action and began to steward, instead of bury, what He had provided. Stepping into the bank that day and talking to the banker to open up that account was the last step in a chain of obedience and follow-through. It was time to accept the fact that I was a steward, not an owner, of the money in my pockets. It was time to sow it into the Lord's Kingdom. That is what had brought me to the bank that day.

After my mental flashback ended, I found the words to answer the banker's question about my five-year plan. With a smile, I told her, "To give it all away." She did not really know what to do with that response, so we moved on. But in my spirit I felt something shift. I could see myself slaying the giant of fear and crossing over my destiny line to the other side, into the land the Lord was calling me to. He was waiting on me, arms open wide, and motioning me to run to Him. What a feeling of victory!

My friend, whether or not you hear Him, the Lord is with you right now whispering the same words of encouragement over your spirit that He did over mine. I can feel the presence of God washing over me to tell you this:

> *The Spirit of breakthrough is here. I Am is with you, motioning for you to cross over your destiny line. Look at the giant of fear. Look him in the eye. And fear not. Now turn your gaze on Jesus. He is the author, He is the perfector of your faith. Follow only Him, and you will win. Simply let go and run. Run to My Son. He is waiting for you on the other side of your destiny line. It is time, says the Lord of Hosts.*

Start with What You Have

It is easy to assume that we do not have to start to steward what God has given us until it is big. We look at what we have now and compare ourselves and our resources to what we hope for in the future, and we tell ourselves—wrongly—that we do not have to be responsible for sowing until there is a big enough harvest to warrant the reaping. But this is not how the Kingdom works. Good stewardship is not stewarding big things well; it is stewarding whatever we have, even if it is little, in a way that honors God and shows obedience to Him.

Just look at David and King Saul. When David stepped onto the battlefield, he had been anointed as king over Israel, but he had not yet been crowned king. In terms of resources, he had next to nothing. What if he had looked at Saul and decided not to take on Goliath because he did not have armor or an important title or because he was so young that he was not even supposed to be on the battlefield in the first place?

Saul already had everything David would one day possess. He was still the king of the nation and the leader of the army in the valley. He had the biggest, most important job in the land. He was the richest and most powerful man in Israel. But he had already lost the anointing of God because he had failed to steward the kingdom according to the Lord's command, and he was losing the battle against Goliath. Saul had abdicated his calling to shepherd God's people.

David, on the other hand, picked up everything he had—a staff, a pouch with rocks in it, a sling, and his mandate from God—and used every bit of it that day on the battlefield. He sowed all he had, and look what God did with that investment.

It is likely that right now you are holding everything you need in order to cross the battle line and enter the promised land of your destiny. What is in your hands right now, not what you wish you had, is exactly what God will use to catapult you to victory over the giant of fear and into His calling for your life.

What Is in Your Hand?

Moses is another clear example of this truth. God appeared to Moses in a burning bush one day while he was tending sheep. Forty years earlier, Moses had fled Egypt and a life in the palace, and now God appeared to him in the form of fire on a bush to tell him He was calling him back to Egypt.

Can you imagine? You are doing your normal day-to-day routine when suddenly you walk out of your house to find the shrub in your front yard is on fire, and coming from it is the audible voice of the living God. What an experience. I would guess God would have my full attention in that case. He certainly had Moses'.

> Now Moses was tending the flock of Jethro his father-in-law, the priest of Midian, and he led the flock to the far side of the wilderness and came to Horeb, the mountain of God. There the angel of the LORD appeared to him in flames of fire from within a bush. Moses saw that though the bush was on fire it did not burn up. So Moses thought, "I will go over and see this strange sight—why the bush does not burn up."
>
> When the Lord saw that he had gone over to look, God called to him from within the bush, "Moses! Moses!"
>
> And Moses said, "Here I am."
>
> "Do not come any closer," God said. "Take off your sandals, for the place where you are standing is holy ground." Then he said, "I am the God of your father, the God of Abraham, the God of Isaac and the God of Jacob." At this, Moses hid his face, because he was afraid to look at God.
>
> Exodus 3:1–6

As if that was not enough to overwhelm a person, God jumped right into His calling on Moses' life. He told Moses of His seemingly impossible plan to free His people from slavery in Egypt, and God told him that one day Moses would return to this place, to this very mountain, to worship God for all that He had done.

> The LORD said, "I have indeed seen the misery of my people in Egypt. I have heard them crying out because of their slave

drivers, and I am concerned about their suffering. So I have come down to rescue them from the hand of the Egyptians and to bring them up out of that land into a good and spacious land, a land flowing with milk and honey—the home of the Canaanites, Hittites, Amorites, Perizzites, Hivites and Jebusites. And now the cry of the Israelites has reached me, and I have seen the way the Egyptians are oppressing them. So now, go. I am sending you to Pharaoh to bring my people the Israelites out of Egypt."

But Moses said to God, "Who am I that I should go to Pharaoh and bring the Israelites out of Egypt?"

And God said, "I will be with you. And this will be the sign to you that it is I who have sent you: When you have brought the people out of Egypt, you will worship God on this mountain."

Exodus 3:7–12

In the light of the burning bush, God brought Moses to the other side of the victory line. Now He was commanding Moses to go back and lead the people over it together.

Moses was terrified. The voice of the Lord was speaking to him audibly through this flaming bush, but the voice of the enemy in Moses' head was twice as loud. He droned on and on about Moses' identity, his authority and his ability. The enemy's voice came out of Moses' mouth in the form of three questions:

1. "Who am I that I should go to Pharaoh and bring the Israelites out of Egypt?" (verse 11). The giant of fear had succeeded in getting Moses to question his identity in God. He did not yet see himself as a steward of God's mandate; instead, he could only see himself as the man who fled the Pharaoh's palace and

his Israelite brothers in disgrace. How could he of all people carry out God's plan?

2. "Suppose I go to the Israelites and say to them, 'The God of your fathers has sent me to you,' and they ask me, 'What is his name?' Then what shall I tell them? . . . What if they do not believe me or listen to me and say, 'The Lord did not appear to you'?" (Exodus 3:13, 4:1). Moses' perception of his own identity was already shaken, so it was short work for the enemy to undermine his authority. Confident he was unqualified, Moses began to question whether or not the Israelites would trust that God had really sent him to them.

3. "Pardon your servant, Lord. I have never been eloquent, neither in the past nor since you have spoken to your servant. I am slow of speech and tongue" (verse 10). In other words, "I'm a terrible public speaker. Why do You want me to speak for You before Pharaoh?" Imagine your greatest weakness. Got it? Now imagine God asks you to put that weakness on display before the entire known world. It makes me tremble just thinking about it. For Moses, being asked to serve as God's mouthpiece revealed perhaps his greatest insecurity: his poor verbal communication skills. The enemy had him convinced he was literally unable to carry out his responsibilities before God.

The Lord is so kind. He knew Moses was afraid. He knew that the giant of fear had gotten inside Moses' head. He also knew that what He was asking of Moses was big. It required him to take immediate action and use the weapons of obedience, faithfulness and stewardship all in one motion. Instead of being irritated or even angry that Moses, His chosen servant, did not trust Him, God responded lovingly to Moses' fears, answering each of his concerns. Then He switched His approach.

What He said next surely caught Moses off guard: "What is that in your hand?" (verse 2). What did God want Moses to see? What was the awe-inspiring instrument of faith to which God directed Moses' attention? What was the tool that would slay the giant of fear in Moses' life and also set the captives free? A staff. Moses' shepherd's rod.

It had been with him every day throughout his forty years in the desert. He had used it to fend off the predators who dared try to take out his sheep. I imagine it was dirty. We are talking real here, so I will guess it even had sheep poop on it.

Seriously, think about that for a moment. That staff was the very evidence the enemy would use to solidify in Moses' mind why he was not qualified to carry out God's plan. And yet, in Moses' hand, it was the instrument God would use to bring His supernatural provision, protection and favor to His people.

Moses' staff would be a sign and a wonder to Pharaoh, to the people, to Moses and to the giant of fear. It was another symbol that God could use any person and anything to bring about His deliverance. And then the inanimate symbol *moved*.

The LORD said, "Throw it on the ground."

Moses threw it on the ground and it became a snake, and he ran from it. Then the LORD said to him, "Reach out your hand and take it by the tail." So Moses reached out and took hold of the snake and it turned back into a staff in his hand. "This," said the LORD, "is so that they may believe that the LORD, the God of their fathers—the God of Abraham, the God of Isaac and the God of Jacob—has appeared to you."

verses 3–5

Moses could have continued to argue with God, but he did not. Yes, God would use his staff later as a sign and a wonder to Pharaoh, but right then, first, the Lord had used it as a sign and a wonder for Moses. The roar of breakthrough began to swell up within Moses in this exchange. His focus began shifting from his fear to courage and from resistance to trust.

God loved Moses, and He gave him the opportunity to realize that when God breathes on something, no matter how small or meaningless we deem it, it can be used for the supernatural. All we have to do is steward it well. In Moses' hands, that staff became the instrument of deliverance for an entire people group.

It was the same staff he held as he led the Israelites out of captivity and to the shoreline of victory, the banks of the impossible. There, once again, the giant of fear positioned himself in opposition to God's mandate and began to tell them all the reasons they could not pass over to the other side of the sea, all the reasons it did not even make sense for them to try. But Moses had come too far at this point to turn back. He knew too much about God's faithfulness. He knew the calling God had given him to steward. So he raised his staff in the air, and he watched as God Almighty parted the Red Sea before him. He lifted up what he had. He used what the Lord deemed relevant and partnered with His leading.

The enemy wants us to fear we are not enough, that we lack the authority or ability to fulfill our calling, that we are ill equipped. But just like He did with Moses, God looks at us, challenging us to use that which is in our hand, what we already have. Stewardship is a weapon against fear because it requires us to understand that we are called to manage what we have, not what we do not have. This shifts our mindset and leads us to certain victory over the giant in our lives.

Do not make the mistake of overlooking what you have already been given, my friend. Allow what you consider to be small and insignificant to become instead a sign and a wonder to you, your family, your community and to the giant of fear. Steward it well and watch as God uses it to catapult you over that destiny line and bring the breakthrough your heart has been longing for.

DECLARE IT

I will stop undermining that which God says is in my hand as a tool to slay the giant of fear. I will steward well what I have been given. I am a champion in Christ!

12

Abide in Christ

And we all, who with unveiled faces contemplate
the Lord's glory, are being transformed into his
image with ever-increasing glory, which comes
from the Lord, who is the Spirit.

2 Corinthians 3:18

The first prophetic word I ever received came when I was fifteen years old. In the months after that incredible encounter I had with the Father when I felt Him wrapping His arms around me and breaking the chains of fear over my life, this word came spilling out on to the page one day as I stewarded my time with the Lord:

I love you, My children. I made you. I created you. You are Mine. Do all that you can for Me. Time is short. The devil wants you to come home with him. I want you to come home with Me. Who will you choose? I will give you peace, love and happiness* with eternal treasures in heaven. The devil will give you only misery, hatred and grief with eternal pain in hell. Who will you choose? I made you. I created you. I need you. Who will you choose? Choose life, not death. I love you. Choose Me, says the Lord.

"Time is short." That is not something you normally hear a fifteen-year-old kid proclaiming, but this word, like all prophetic words, did not come from me. While it certainly applied to my life at the time, it has continued to hold significance for me as I have gotten older. This word has been a living organism throughout my entire adult life and still carries the same relevance as the day the Lord first spoke it to me in May of 1998. That is because it contains an important truth: God is always calling His beloved into greater stewardship of the time we have been given here on the earth.

Time is one of our most precious resources. This side of eternity, it is finite. Choosing to spend our time one way means choosing not to spend it on something else. Whether we think of it in these terms or not, what we do with the time we are given each day, week and year is up to us. God is asking us—challenging us—to remember that those choices matter and to decide well. Will we choose to steward our time in pursuit of our created purpose, or will we choose to sow our time to our flesh?

For those of us who choose to live our life for the Kingdom, it can be tempting to assume that working for the Kingdom is the holiest way of stewarding our time. It is sacred, but it is not our highest charge. Jesus said the greatest command is not that we do things for Him but rather that we love Him with all our heart. Sometimes being a good steward

*The Holy Spirit inserted the word *joy* in this series later in my life.

of our hours means resting at the feet of Christ, growing in intimacy with Him. We must not become so busy serving God that we forget to love Him well.

Love Casts Out All Fear

Remember, we learned from David that his obedience and faithfulness grew from his close walk with God. Because David loved the Lord, he was empowered to obey Him without being asked. His absolute trust in God's faithfulness gave him the courage to follow through even in the face of fear. And David's adoration for the Father motivated him to invest everything he had—even his life, if need be—into the call God placed on his life. This chain of actions began and was sustained by time spent with the Lord.

David knew well that being a good steward of his time began and ended with abiding in God. In our fast-paced culture, this is a hard lesson but an important one. It is part of our God-given calling to steward our time by spending it at Jesus' feet. It is our job to abide in Him, rest in Him and worship Him with our attention and our every breath.

The enemy uses fear not only to try to prevent us from serving the mission and call of God but also to prevent us from abiding in Him. He works hard to distract us with the fear that time will run out in our day and we will not be as productive as we wanted to be. He tries to derail us with the fear that we have to run like hamsters in a wheel to get what we need in this earth. He wants us to hustle and grind so we forget that Jesus is waiting on us to cast our gaze on Him and remember Him.

Jesus longs for us to have communion with Him, to reflect on His blood shed on the cross for us and to think about His broken body hanging there on the cross for us. He bore all our sin, our shame and our guilt as He awaited the wrath of the Father to be poured out upon Himself.

> But he was pierced for our transgressions, he was crushed for our iniquities; the punishment that brought us peace was on him, and by his wounds we are healed. We all, like sheep, have gone astray, each of us has turned to our own way; and the LORD has laid on him the iniquity of us all.
>
> Isaiah 53:5–6

This is what gives us the victory over fear, my friend: the image of Jesus on the cross, smitten by man, forsaken by the Father and bearing the full punishment for your sin and mine. When we fail to steward our time with Christ, we run the risk of losing sight of what He did for us, of the love that "drives out fear" of all kinds in our lives forever (1 John 4:18).

> There is no fear in love. But perfect love drives out fear, because fear has to do with punishment. The one who fears is not made perfect in love.
>
> 1 John 4:18

We move into greater glory and victory as we grow in our fellowship with Jesus and His sufferings. It is His plan for us to abide in Him, and He in us, and stewardship leads us into this fellowship. Notice this progression from the mouth of Jesus Christ:

> I am the vine; you are the branches. If you remain in me and I in you, you will bear much fruit; apart from me you can do nothing. If you do not remain in me, you are like a branch that is thrown away and withers; such branches are picked

162

up, thrown into the fire and burned. If you remain in me and my words remain in you, ask whatever you wish, and it will be done for you. This is to my Father's glory, that you bear much fruit, showing yourselves to be my disciples.

John 15:5–8

Stewarding our time well by abiding in Him—this is key to bearing fruit in our lives. And it is cyclical. The more we abide in Him, the more fruit we bear. The more fruit we bear, the more our lives overflow with Him and our love increases. This love leads us to obey His commands to love Him more, which produces faithfulness and draws us closer to His heart. As this happens, we crave time at His feet, which we then begin to steward, and the cycle continues.

It all begins with an intentional decision to prioritize set-apart time with the Lord. Let go today, my friend, and fall back into the arms of your beautiful Savior. He ripped through eternity to get to you. Reach back today. Tell Him how much you love Him, and feel His perfect peace wash over you right now as a blanket, as the robe of righteousness He drapes on you, His beloved.

There Is Going to Be a Wedding

Recently I had a prophetic dream that reminded me just how important it is to prioritize time with God. It all started in a board meeting of sorts.

Sunlight beamed through the floor-to-ceiling windows as I entered the room and walked over to the large oval table in its center. Scanning my surroundings, I realized I was not in a room at all but rather in the lobby of a beautiful hotel. Strangely, the lobby was empty, except for the handful of men sitting around the table. In the dream, I recognized them as leaders.

As I approached the table, they motioned for me to sit down in the only empty chair, which happened to be at the head of the table. That is when I realized they had been waiting for me. I somehow knew they were waiting to hear what I had to say. There was a very serious matter regarding some teaching that had gone on in the church, and this meeting was assembled to hear my thoughts and concerns, since I had not weighed in on it yet.

When I sat down, one of the pastors stood up above the rest and began to pray. His volume grew louder and louder, and the intensity of his prayer also increased significantly as he went on. At some point, he even began waving his arms at me as he asked God to speak through me and bring clarity on this issue. His body language grew hostile, and his tone angry. There was tension in the room. The giant of fear had stepped inside.

Suddenly, as the pastor's prayer was escalating to another level, a group of joyful bridesmaids entered the room. They were wearing silk robes and began to do one another's hair and makeup for the wedding. Some had curlers in their hair. Others were applying makeup. Seemingly oblivious to our presence, or the pastor's tone, the bridesmaids overtook the emptiness, surrounding our table with their preparations and joy.

Finally the pastor stopped praying and turned to the bridesmaids. "What are you doing here?" he asked angrily. "Can you not see we are having a meeting?"

One of the women, curling iron still in hand, replied, "We got this all approved. We are supposed to be here. See?" She laid the iron down in order to reveal a signed legal document confirming their arrangement to use this space for the wedding they were preparing for. The document was ancient in appearance and was unrolled like a handwritten parchment scroll. At the bottom was a signature in a deep red ink that looked like blood.

But the pastor would not even look at it. He just grew angrier and began to shout, "I don't care. You have to go."

The bridesmaids tried explaining again, still full of joy. "But we are supposed to be here. There's going to be a wedding!"

He would not listen. He cut them off. "Just go," he said. "Go!"

Deflated, the beautiful bridesmaids quickly cleaned up their things and left the room.

The pastor then finished his prayer and sat down. "Okay, we are ready," he said, turning to me. "What do you have to say?"

I was stunned. My heart was pounding in my chest. What I had just encountered was astonishing. When I opened my mouth to speak, I felt tears welling up in my eyes. I looked around the table at each of the leaders, and all I could say was, "Don't you understand? There's going to be a wedding!" That is when I woke up.

My friend, here is the truth: Time is short, and there is going to be a wedding. Our life on this earth is meant as preparation for the great wedding between Jesus, the Bridegroom, and us, His bride. The lessons we learn, the time we spend in His presence to grow in wisdom and be made to look more and more like Christ—it all leads up to this glorious union of the bride and the Bridegroom.

This life will give us much trouble. Jesus told us it would. We will face trials and fears and failures and messes. We

have been over that in this book already. But let us not forget we are living on the side of the cross where we can take
heart and be of good cheer. Even in the midst of hardship,
we should live joyfully, as a bride preparing for a wedding,
rejoicing in time we have with our Lord now, as well as what
awaits us in heaven.

You are not here by accident or chance. You are here on
purpose, divine purpose. And this makes the devil terrified.
He prowls about like a lion seeking whom he may devour. He
wants to devour your hopes and your dreams, robbing you
of the joy available to you as the bride of Christ. He wants
to hold you in a prison of your own worry, fear, shame and
pain, and all for his own gain. But as the bride of Christ, you
can refrain from the game and bring Jesus fame by running
full speed ahead.

The more you learn about how to steward your time well,
the quieter the voice of fear will be in your life. Reach into
your pouch now and pull out that smooth stone of stewardship. Examine it. Does it look like it can slay the giant of fear?
It can. And it will. You need simply use it. Let your arm be
the catalyst for victory today as you release that stone into
the forehead of your opposer and rise in victory.

DECLARE IT

*I am the bride of Christ, and I will steward my time
in His presence well—abiding in Christ, bearing fruit
with my life and rejoicing because there is going to be
a wedding. I am a champion in Christ!*

PART 5

RELEASE
YOUR ROAR

13

Be of Good Courage

For God did not give us a spirit of timidity or
cowardice or fear, but [He has given us a spirit]
of power and of love and of sound judgment and
personal discipline [abilities that result in a calm,
well-balanced mind and self-control].

2 Timothy 1:7 AMP

I heard someone say the other day, "Fear is the opposite
of faith." I might have amen'd that if I were not in the
throes of writing a book about fear. This assignment
on my life makes me very sensitive to the details of any message or teaching about fear. The Holy Spirit highlighted this
statement when I heard it, so I inquired of the Lord about
it. "Is this correct, Lord? Is fear the opposite of faith?" The
more I pressed in, the clearer the answer became. Fear is not
the opposite of faith but rather of courage. When we fear,

it is because we lack courage, which gives us perseverance in the face of fear.

When we are courageous, fear does not have a voice in our decisions. We proceed regardless. We press on toward the mark, eyes fixed on Jesus. He is the author and perfector of our faith. As we wield our weapons of obedience, faithfulness and stewardship, we grow bolder and develop more and more courage. Over time, it becomes easier to ignore the voice of the enemy and carry on in victorious pursuit of our divine purpose.

Fear Motivated King Saul

It should come as no surprise that David was a man of great courage. As a representation of our spirit man, David walked out his love for God powerfully, even in the face of fear. His actions and attitudes stand in stark contrast to those of King Saul, who lacked courage. Saul allowed fear to consume him and direct his steps time and time again.

Israel's first king did not wield the weapons of obedience, faithfulness and stewardship. Quite the opposite. He had a habit of acting impulsively, of relying more on his own instinct and ideas than on the Lord's counsel. Ultimately, it cost Saul his anointing.

The Scriptures tell us that Saul's pattern of fear-based decision-making began almost as soon as Samuel anointed him king over Israel. When Saul returned from that anointing, he ran into his uncle at the high place and immediately lied about where he had been and what he had been doing.

> Now Saul's uncle asked him and his servant, "Where have you been?"

"Looking for the donkeys," he said. "But when we saw they were not to be found, we went to Samuel."

Saul's uncle said, "Tell me what Samuel said to you."

Saul replied, "He assured us that the donkeys had been found." But he did not tell his uncle what Samuel had said about the kingship.

1 Samuel 10:14–16

Why would Saul withhold such information? Fear. Even though God had touched Saul's heart and anointed him as king, Saul still had a choice to make—and he chose to listen to the wrong voice. He inclined his ear to fear instead of courage, and it established a precedent in his life and reign.

Not long after this exchange with his uncle, Samuel gathered the Israelites together to announce who God had chosen to be their king. Terrified, Saul hid in a supply closet.

Samuel summoned the people of Israel to the LORD at Mizpah and said to them, "This is what the LORD, the God of Israel, says: 'I brought Israel up out of Egypt, and I delivered you from the power of Egypt and all the kingdoms that oppressed you.' But you have now rejected your God, who saves you out of all your disasters and calamities. And you have said, 'No, appoint a king over us.' So now present yourselves before the LORD by your tribes and clans."

When Samuel had all Israel come forward by tribes, the tribe of Benjamin was taken by lot. Then he brought forward the tribe of Benjamin, clan by clan, and Matri's clan was taken. Finally Saul son of Kish was taken. But when they looked for him, he was not to be found. So they inquired further of the LORD, "Has the man come here yet?" And the LORD said, "Yes, he has hidden himself among the supplies."

1 Samuel 10:17–22

At the very moment when he was to step into his anointing, Saul was overcome by the giant of fear. Why? Perhaps it was the fact that no one had ever been king before. It was a first for the nation of Israel, and there was a lot of expectation on Saul's shoulders. I am sure it felt heavy, especially since Saul lacked an understanding of stewardship. He likely sensed the weight of his calling and wrongly assumed God meant for him to own it instead of steward it. Without the courage that comes from connectedness with the Father, the voice of the enemy was simply too loud.

In fact, Saul never seemed to learn how to silence it in order to hear and obey the voice of the Lord. Later, before one critical battle against the Philistines, Saul and the Israelites were so afraid that they "were quaking with fear" (1 Samuel 13:7). Some of the soldiers hid in caves and wells, and others deserted the army entirely, crossing the Jordan into an adjacent land. Saul remained, but he began to grow anxious that Samuel, the priest, had not arrived on the battlefield to perform the offering to the Lord. In conscious disobedience to the Law of God, Saul offered up the burnt offering and fellowship offering himself, and with a fearful heart (see verses 7–10).

Just as he finished making the offering, Samuel arrived, and Saul went out to greet him. "What have you done?" asked Samuel. Saul replied, "When I saw that the men were scattering, and that you did not come at the set time, and that the Philistines were assembling at Mikmash, I thought, 'Now the Philistines will come down against me at Gilgal, and I have not sought the LORD's favor.' So I felt compelled to offer the burnt offering."

"You have done a foolish thing," Samuel said. "You have not kept the command the LORD your God gave you; if you had, he would have established your kingdom over Israel for all time. But now your kingdom will not endure; the LORD has sought out a man after his own heart and appointed him ruler of his people, because you have not kept the LORD's command."

Saul knew it was not his place to present those offerings before the Lord. He chose to circumvent God's established order not so much because he lacked faith but because he lacked courage. That day, Samuel told Saul that God was looking for his replacement, someone who would seek His heart and prioritize obedience, faithfulness and stewardship even over his own life. God's choice? David.

David's love for God gave him the courage to live out his calling well. Even when he failed—and he sure did fail at times, didn't he?—he showed remorse and repentance. He passed on the wisdom he gained through times of trial and great pressing to his children, including Solomon, who became, thanks to God's anointing on his life, the wisest man who ever lived. Solomon went on to write the book of Proverbs, in which he recorded these lessons Saul would have done well to learn:

> "There is a way that appears to be right, but in the end it leads to death."
>
> Proverbs 14:12

> "Trust in the Lord with all your heart and lean not on your own understanding; in all your ways submit to him, and he will make your paths straight."
>
> Proverbs 3:5–6

Let us remember that even in the chaos and confusion of our battle with the giant of fear, God's way is always better than ours. Our best attempt to preserve our life will only cause us to lose it, if it means acting in disobedience to the Lord or falling short of faithfulness and stewardship. Even when it seems too hard, even when we fear the battle may kill us, we must know: Jesus is always with us, protecting us from harm and leading us into the victory He bought with His own blood.

Fear of God Builds Courage

My friend, God is looking for a people who, simply put, will not take matters into their own hands, as Saul did. He is looking for those who are willing to do what might seem foolish to the world if it means they are acting in the fear of the Lord, which is the beginning of wisdom and of courage.

The fear of the Lord frees us from a life of people-pleasing, a life of fearing man and a life of fearing outcomes. It brings us into a level of trust in the Lord that many will never understand. That trust liberates us to operate in a way the world will not understand. It will not make sense, except to those who are functioning in the same manner, following the voice of their Shepherd.

Why would it make sense for David to reject Saul's armor? It did not make sense. But David feared God more than he feared hurting Saul's feelings by rejecting his offer to wear his armor and bear his sword. He feared God, not Goliath. He feared God more than death, so he stepped up to the battle line with courage.

Did it make sense for Moses to lead the Israelites to the shoreline of the Red Sea with Pharaoh's army on their heels? Of course not. There was at least one other, more direct route out of Egypt. Moses knew that well because he had already taken it twice—once when he fled from Egypt and next upon his return to free his people. So why would Moses lead an entire race of people to a dead end? Because God said so. Because he had already encountered God in the desert, and he feared the Lord more than the soldiers' swords. Because he was filled with courage.

And what about Esther? Did it make sense for her to risk her life to go before the king when she had not been invited? Not in the natural. But in the spirit, it was the only option. Esther's fear of the living God gave her courage in the face of the enemy's attempt to make her fear her death.

You do not have anything to fear when your motive is serving your King, honoring His heart and doing what He says. Rest in Him, abide in Him, and He will fill your heart so full of courage that there will be no room for the enemy's shouts.

Alpha, Omega and in Between

The Bible tells us that God is the Alpha and the Omega. He is the beginning and the end, and everything in between. The story line of humanity was written by God Himself and continues to unfold according to His plan. The question is, Do you trust Him enough to lead you into His desired outcome for your life? Will you fear the Lord and walk in courage even when it seems like God does not have a plan, much less a good one?

My friend Sula's life story reads like a novel you are unsure will have a happy ending, but thankfully, it does. As a child, she was the victim of sexual abuse that left her traumatized. Broken and unequipped to process what had happened to her in her most formative years, Sula turned to drugs and alcohol to cope. Eventually, she hit rock bottom. In the midst of an attempt to take her own life, Sula had an encounter with Jesus. He appeared to her just as the life was leaving her body and showed her multitudes of people. He said to her, "If you die, who will reach them?" Miraculously, she survived and made a full recovery.

Though she had this experience with the Lord, she did not have anyone in her life to disciple her. Once her physical wounds healed, she continued down the same path she was on to numb the pain of her past: the parties, the drugs, the drinking, the men. This was the only life she knew.

Then, just when things seemed they could not get any worse, Sula was lured into the world of sex trafficking. She was twenty years old and pursuing modeling, so when the invitation to work as a model in another country arose, she did not question it. She felt she was living the dream, until the dream became a prison. For three weeks Sula was held in another country, having been purchased as a gift by a billionaire magnate. The darkness she walked into could have and likely would have killed her, had she not gotten an idea: She requested to fly home to handle a few family matters before she settled into her new home. I believe the Lord gave her that idea and blinded the eyes of her captors so they would allow her to go, believing she would return. Of course, she never did. Miraculously she was free.

After so much trauma, things seemed to improve. She became engaged to a wealthy African prince, who treated her to thirty-thousand-dollar shopping sprees on Rodeo Drive in California, private jets and a life of luxury. I imagine she thought, *Why should I not take this opportunity to be happy, after so much pain? Why would I not relish being pampered and enjoy the good life being offered to me?* Yet, amidst all the wealth and the attention—and the opportunity to become a real-life princess—Sula could not shake the overwhelming feeling that she was missing something. Inexplicably, she felt empty.

The more she thought about it, the more it seemed that nagging sense of emptiness could be related to the encounter she had with Jesus when she attempted suicide. Still, with no other knowledge of truth and her past trauma unhealed, Sula tried to reinterpret Jesus' message to fit her desire for comfort and security. She told herself that as a princess, she could reach the multitudes Jesus called her to serve. Surely marrying the prince was the pathway to accomplishing her purpose, the very reason she had survived up to this point. This reasoning only took her deeper into a lifestyle that could not satisfy.

Then one life-altering day it was as though a lightbulb went on in her spirit, and she saw all that she had through a new lens. She looked around at all her expensive designer clothes and shoes and bags and wanted nothing to do with them anymore. Sula cried out to the Lord, "I would rather live in a cardboard box and be in Your will than lead my own life, miserable in luxury. I surrender my life to You, Jesus. I give it all to You. Everything else is nothing. It's garbage. It's dung." She gave away all her fancy possessions and walked away from her relationship with the prince. She gave her life over to the Lord once and for all.

This was the moment Sula moved from glory to glory, from death to life and from operating in the flesh to being led by the Spirit. Knowing her today, you would look at her and think she is one of those few who has not gone through anything in her life. She overflows with the joy of the Lord. She beams with the light of Christ. She is now married with two beautiful children, and she and her husband pastor a thriving church in Destin, Florida. She has learned to wield obedience, faithfulness and stewardship expertly against unimaginable fear, and it has given her courage like I have never witnessed in another person.

At any point in her journey, it would have been easy for Sula to say, "God has abandoned me. He does not care that I am in pain. He does not have a plan for my life, or if He does, it is for someone else's benefit. He probably does not even see me." But Sula did not give up on God. She did not walk with Him, but she knew of His goodness, and it sustained her. He had reached out to her in her most desperate moment, and she trusted—even when she was living far from Him—that His plan for her was both sure and good. He had begun a "good work" in her, and He would "carry it on to completion" (Philippians 1:6). God was faithful, and so was she. She pressed in to intimacy with Him, and as a result, she has seen countless lives changed forever, just like Jesus promised her so many years ago.*

Love Is Greater Than Fear

"You will seek me and find me when you seek me with all your heart. I will be found by you," declares the LORD.

Jeremiah 29:13

Wherever you are in your journey with the Lord—beginning, middle or end—God is with you. He sees you, and He sees what strikes fear in your heart. He has drawn a destiny line on the path in front of you and has laid out a plan that will carry you safely over to the other side. He has prepared

*For more information about Sula's incredible story, visit her website, sulaskiles.com.

everything for you, but it will take courage on your part to cross it, and that courage grows from love.

God can do anything. He could have designed man to wake up one day and just know everything there is to know about Himself and about creation. But instead, He designed man to need daily communion with Him in relationship. That intimacy is what will sustain you when the enemy does his best to drown out the voice of God in your life. It is what will give you boldness when the giant of fear positions himself between you and your God-given destiny. God has given you all the weapons you will need to take him down, but He has also given you Himself. When you seek Him and find Him, when you draw near to Him and abide in Him, you will become both fearless and victorious.

DECLARE IT

I will not trade my weapons of obedience, faithfulness and stewardship for disobedience and timidity. Rather, I will be bold and courageous in pursuit of Jesus. I am a champion in Christ!

14

The Roar of Breakthrough

The righteous are as bold as a lion.

Proverbs 28:1

Let's return to the Valley of Elah one last time. I want you to picture the battlefield again in vivid detail. Can you see it? On one side, the army of Israel waits, gripped in fear, and on the other side of the battle line is Goliath. He is huge, loud and ferocious. His taunts are relentless. With each new word from his mouth, the Israelites cower yet further. But I ask you, what has been stolen from this army? Their food? No. Their armor? Nope. Their health? Not yet. They had been threatened but unharmed. What about their hope? What about their joy? Their courage? Yes, yes and yes.

By undercutting the Israelites' authority and identity, this belligerent giant had apprehended the hope of an entire army. He had managed to steal joy from this entire group of men, and it produced a domino effect that caused them to lose their courage. Their bodies were clad in armor for battle, but their souls were stripped bare, vulnerable. Even with sword in hand, they were utterly defenseless.

Can you relate to this feeling of being stripped bare from the inside out, riddled with fear, hope shattered, your joy no longer existent? I certainly can. If someone had asked me a few years back, "What happened to your joy?" I would likely have looked at him like he had lost his mind. Internally I would have responded, "*My joy? You don't know what I'm going through right now. You have no clue what has gone on in my life. I have a good reason to be afraid and devoid of joy.*"

Is this ringing any bells for you? I do not know what is going on in your life right now or what you have been through. But what I do know is this: God loves you and has a plan for your life. He created you for a purpose. You can get your hopes up today, my friend. Allow the joy of the Lord to rise within you, regardless of your circumstances right now. The joy of the Lord is your strength—not the joy of your circumstances. Allow the fire of His presence and His great love for you to refine you today. Do not let the enemy rob you of that power just because you are going through a battle right now.

Do not let the enemy rob you of your destiny, either. Remember, when Jesus died, His death broke the curse we were under and cut the head off of fear once and for all. Instead of a living, breathing Goliath, an insurmountable enemy, our foe is no more than a headless, flailing monster. My friend Jeremiah Yancy said one time, "Headless fear cannot talk, intimidate, threaten or stand in the way." But I can tell you this: It will try. In fact, many of us got so used to the echo of fear's cries in our lives that we forgot the power of the cross freed us from its influence and intimidation. All this time, we have been cowering before a dead foe.

That ends today. The Bible says you are made to go "from glory to glory" (2 Corinthians 3:18 NKJV). This transformation is ongoing. How do you suppose you access this greater glory? You cross over. You lay hold of the promise, slaying the giant of fear each time. You certainly cannot do that if you are backpedaling. You cannot even do it standing still, holding your ground. You must advance. Friend, it is time to claim your promised land.

The Enemy Fears You

Here is the thing: There will always be a giant standing at the battle line of your destiny. It is simply the truth. The devil will always place his best and biggest giants there to mock you, intimidate you and scare you into giving up. Why? Because he knows what is on the other side of that line. He knows the blessings that lie over there on the other side for you. He knows your promised land is full of life and abundance and fresh hope and joy. The enemy will do anything to stop you because once you cross over, you become the giant *he* fears.

Every time a child of God crosses over the battle line, past Goliath, to the land of his or her destiny, that child becomes stronger and harder for the enemy to defeat. When the roar of breakthrough erupts from the hearts of God's children, the enemy becomes paralyzed with terror. He becomes afraid—of you and of me. That is why he does not want us realizing who we are and whose we are. He does not want us walking in victory. He wants us backing down, running scared and wandering aimlessly around the same land we have dwelled in for years.

Remember the Israelites. The army of God was so focused on preventing Goliath from coming over to their side that they lost track of the fact that their sole purpose and mandate from heaven was to cross over and take the land. They lost sight of who they were fighting for and who was fighting the battle through them. They even forgot about the Red Sea parting and the walls of Jericho tumbling down. They did not realize that right in this moment in time they were being written into the story line of heaven, the narrative of God's eternal story. They needed a reminder. And thankfully, they got one. Just when they thought all was lost, a shepherd boy walked on the scene and saw things a different way.

Has this happened in your life? Have you forgotten how God parted the Red Sea of your hopeless situation all those years ago? Or how the walls of despair came tumbling down by the hand of God in your family situation? Close your eyes right now and reflect. Remember the wonders of the Lord in your life. Reflect on His goodness. Tell Him this:

Thank You, Father, for rescuing me from the muck and the mire. Thank You for pulling me out of the pit of despair and setting my feet upon the solid rock. Thank You, Jesus, for saving me. Thank You, Father, for parting the seas of despair and hopelessness in my life. Thank You for Your joy, which is my strength, and for giving me hope and a future.

There is a line in front of you today, my friend. This is the line that the ugly giant of fear has guarded, trying to get you to run far, far away from. I want you to imagine yourself like David today, filled with courage and faith, stepping boldly up to your battle line. You are carrying the weapons God has

184

already placed in your hands—obedience, faithfulness and stewardship—and you are confident and bold. You know the outcome of this battle, even before it has begun, because you know your God, who fights for you, and "you need only to be still" (Exodus 14:14). You are a champion in Christ!

Your Promised Land Awaits

As you prepare to launch your attack on your enemy, I want you to think about those five stones David carried up to the battle line. They were smooth. The rough edges had been smoothed down by the continual flow of water running over them. This is exactly what occurs in our hearts as we are washed in the river of life flowing from the side of the Lamb. As we immerse ourselves in His presence daily, allowing Him to refine us, He works out all our rough edges. He purifies our hearts.

You see, it is the pure heart that drives the stones to the target, a heart humble enough to declare in boldness to the enemy:

> You come against me with sword and spear and javelin, *but I come against you in the name of the* LORD *Almighty*, the God of the armies of Israel, whom you have defied. *This day the* LORD *will deliver you into my hands, and I'll strike you down and cut off your head.*
>
> 1 Samuel 17:45, emphasis added

Can you hear it? Can you hear the roar of breakthrough bellowing out of David's heart through his mouth as he locked eyes with his opponent? He was carrying only that which He already possessed, and yet there was no shrinking back. No hesitation. There was only courage and assurance in the Lord, whom he represented that day in battle. David stepped up to the battle line and decreed this giant's fate, as well as the restoration of God's name, which the giant of fear had defiled.

> This very day I will give the carcasses of the Philistine army to the birds and the wild animals, and the whole world will know that there is a God in Israel. *All those gathered here will know that it is not by sword or spear that the Lord saves; for the battle is the Lord's, and he will give all of you into our hands.*
>
> 1 Samuel 17:46–47, emphasis added

The Philistine moved in close, but David surged forward in victory to take him down.

> As the Philistine moved closer to attack him, David ran quickly toward the battle line to meet him. Reaching into his bag and taking out a stone, he slung it and struck the Philistine on the forehead. The stone sank into his forehead, and he fell face down on the ground. So David triumphed over the Philistine with a sling and a stone; without a sword in his hand he struck down the Philistine and killed him. David ran and stood over him. He took hold of the Philistine's sword and drew it from the sheath. After he killed him, he cut off his head with the sword.
>
> 1 Samuel 17:48–51

Just like that, the veil of fear was torn in two. The army of the Lord was released to surge forward into their promised land, the land of their destiny, the land the devil worked very hard at preventing them from accessing. The roar of breakthrough bellowed from within the army of the Lord as their identity was restored. Their authority as champions grew with every stride.

Then the men of Israel and Judah surged forward with a shout and pursued the Philistines to the entrance of Gath and to the gates of Ekron.

1 Samuel 17:52

When David and the Israelites crossed their own destiny line, they released the roar of breakthrough that had risen within them. I imagine it echoed back and forth throughout the valley as the army surged forward into the land God had prepared for them. The pounding of their feet must have shaken the very gates of hell.

Now, today, your feet will do no less. You are in the Lord's army, and it is time for you to release your roar of breakthrough and surge forward beyond the battle line. Your promised land awaits!

Your Time Is Now

I want you to imagine now that you are carrying your own smooth stone in your hand as you advance closer and closer to the battle line of your destiny. Do you see the giant of fear before you? Your enemy will step toward you. He will shout louder than ever before. But this time, you know what to do. You are ready, and the roar of breakthrough will soon be released from your lips. It is time.

My friend, the Lord is saying this to you today:

"It is time to rise. Pick up your stones of obedience, faithfulness and stewardship and run the race I have marked out for you with perseverance. Fix your eyes on My Son, for He is the one who will empower you to be all that I have created you to be. Draw near to Me,

187

and I will set you free from the grip of fear and anxiety. I love you, My child. My eyes are on you. I am saying to you now, I am proud of you. You have come so far. You have seen so much. My heart aches that you draw near Me, and I you. So shed your grave clothes now, for I am calling you forth. Arise. Shine. And allow the glory of My Son to radiate from you now and forevermore," says the Lord Almighty.

The prison bars of fear that have held you back are now open wide. You are ready and released to step into your destiny unopposed, the roar of breakthrough now surging forth from your heart. My friend, fall to your knees today right this moment as you read this final decree from the Lord.

Release Your Roar

My friend, God is calling His army to arise,
To lift up our faces,
Stepping into His graces,
Roaring and surging—breaking into new places.
He is saying to you now,

"My child, it is time for you to run.
To surge forward with My Son.
Be 'all in' for the One.

"The giant of fear is no more.
Jesus decreed through His roar
Of breakthrough on the cross
The giant of fear has officially lost.

"Fear has no head *and* no voice.
You have been granted the choice
To listen to Me
As I have set you free,
So step into this reality: Jesus is your victory.

188

"Empowered by love,
All of heaven above
Is watching and waiting and cheering you on.
The giant of fear's influence is gone!
So now it is time for you to step into the new
As you release your roar of breakthrough,"
Says the Lord.

Friend, I can hear the sound of victory arising
As we march boldly forward with our King.
He is the author, the perfector.
He is what all this has been for.

Bubbling up from the ashes of all you have walked
    through,
The fire and the pain, all for His Name.
The Lord of Hosts now charges you
To release your roar of breakthrough!
It is time to surge forth into the new
And realize the following statement as true:
That headless giant of fear—now fears you.

There is victory on the other side of your roar. The time is now to throw caution to the wind and be all-in for Jesus and all-in for the Kingdom and God's will for this earth. You are His messenger. You are His ambassador. You are His image-bearer. You have been released to roar, so roar and surge forward toward the destiny God has been preparing for you since the dawn of time. What is that in your hand? It is your three supernatural weapons to slay the giant of fear: obedience, faithfulness and stewardship. Wield them now as you roar, "I am a champion in Christ!"

Acknowledgments

I want to acknowledge:

My husband, Donovan, for the sacrifices you make so that I can do what God has called me to do in writing books. You are my hero. I love you so much.

My children, for sacrificing precious time with Mommy while I tucked away to write. May God bless you and keep you and His face ever shine upon you, my little loves.

My sisters in Christ: Mary Wells, Christina Walden, Liz Pitman and Rebecca Siler, for the prayers you prayed and the battles you fought in the spirit as you covered me in prayer during this intense writing process.

My amazing family: parents, grandparents, brothers and sisters, who never cease covering me in prayer and supporting my every dream. I thank God for you.

My dad, for the life you live, slaying the giant of fear with your every step of obedience, faithfulness and stewardship. You modeled this message so that I could write about it. Thank you for raising me to think and for teaching me to stand firm upon the solid rock of Christ. I will always look up to you in admiration and deep respect.

And as always, I acknowledge my Savior and best friend, Jesus Christ. He empowers me in my weakness, making me strong. This book is a love offering to my Jesus, without whom this book could not have been written.

Krissy Nelson has a vision for you to see yourself the way God sees you. She carries a passion to release life and hope into your heart so you can walk in all that you were created for. Krissy is a published author and TV show host who travels to speak into the call of God on people's lives. The greatest fruit of Krissy's life is found at home, with her husband and their two treasured children. Learn more at www.krissynelson.com.